BEYOND THE MAP OF
FIVEHEAD AND SWELL

BEYOND THE MAP OF FIVEHEAD AND SWELL

Compiled by members of the
Fivehead Parish Map Committee

Contributors
Shirley Benet
Margaret Curtis
Pauline English
Anne Forward
Joan Greenshields
Helen Hanney
Colin Hight
John Hoover
Paul McManaway
Paul Northcott
Wendy Swinburn
Lesley Tucker
Betty Wheller

The committee would also like to thank the many residents for their contributions, photographs, and sketches.

FIVEHEAD AND SWELL PARISH MAP PRESS

First Published 1999
All rights reserved. No reproduction
permitted without the prior permission
of the publishers.
Fivehead and Swell Parish Map Press
ISBN 0 9537655 0 4

Printed in England by
AA Sotheran Ltd, Redcar

Contents

Introduction	1
The Parish Church of St Martin	1
Fivehead Baptist Church	12
Langford Manor	21
Cathanger	23
Old buildings in Fivehead	28
Events and life in Fivehead and Swell	39
Societies and Clubs	48
Natural History	60
A short history of Swell, in Somerset	78
Conclusion	87

Foreword

This book was compiled by the Parish Map Committee following publication of the Parish Map of Fivehead and Swell in May 1997. The response to the map had been tremendous and much information could not be included on the map.

The committee would like to thank all residents, past and present, who showed such enthusiasm for the project and encouraged us to keep going. As chairman of the project I would also like to thank the committee for their support through the four years it has taken to complete. The committee would also like to thank Somerset Rural Development Area Community Chest for their support in the form of a grant towards the publication of the book.

Wendy Swinburn

Other committee members:-
Shirley Benet, Margaret Curtis, Pauline English, Ann Forward, Joan Greenshields, Helen Hanney, Colin Hight, John Hoover, Paul McManaway, Paul Northcott, Marina Saint, Lesley Tucker and Valerie Wathew.

Maps are available at a cost of £5.00
Plus £1.70 postage and packing.
Cheques payable to:
"The Parish Map of Fivehead and Swell"

Send to:
Parish Map Project.
Webbers, Fivehead,
Taunton, Somerset TA3 6PT

INTRODUCTION

The parish of Fivehead and Swell, situated 9 miles from Taunton and 20 miles from Yeovil, in the heart of Somerset, lies on a ridge of land which stretches from Langport to the Blackdown Hills. The ridge overlooks Sedgemoor, part of the Somerset Levels, to the north, and The Vale of Isles, to the south. The villages of Fivehead and Swell lies on the south slopes of this wooded ridge.

The very earliest settlement in Fivehead was a cluster of wattle and daub dwellings with cruck beams and thatched roofs. There would have been holes in the roofs for smoke to escape from the fires inside. The serfs and villeins who occupied them were entirely self-supporting and had little connection with the outside world. The only roads were cattle tracks which led north to Sedgemoor for the summer grazing and south for access to the river. The road from Taunton to Langport was South Drove which by-passed Fivehead. Traces of ancient dwellings can still be found along its length and there are adzed beams at Lower Listock and a cruck beam at Squirrelmead Cottage which date back to the 14th Century.

Fivehead is given the following entry in the Domesday Book under 21 (Lands held by Roger of Courseulles):
Bertram holds Fivehead from Roger. Aldred held it before 1066; it paid tax for 1½ hides. Land for two ploughs.
Lordship; one plough; two slaves; 1 hide and 1 virgate.
Four smallholders who have 1 virgate.
Meadow, 15 acres; woodlands, 20 acres; two cattle, fifteen pigs, forty sheep, thirty goats.
The true value was 30 shillings; now 40 shillings.

In the process of time, Fivehead and Cathanger seem to have changed hands and the Manor and Advowson of Fivehead passed to the Abbot of Muchelney with whom it remained until the Dissolution; the Advowson is the right to nominate clergy to an ecclesiastical benefice. *(Cartuleries of Muchelney & Athelney Abbey - Som. Records Soc.)*

THE PARISH CHURCH OF ST MARTIN

Introduction

This ancient church, listed Grade I, parts of which date from the 13th century, probably stands on the site of an earlier one.

The church is dedicated to St Martin, the Roman soldier who gave half his cloak to a starving beggar and was later made Bishop of Tours. This dedication was a popular one with early Christians at the time. The church celebrates the Patronal Festival for St Martin on the Sunday nearest 4th July, the date of his consecration as Bishop.

The church registers date from 1654 but records exist in the Hugo Ms. in the British Museum of incumbents before that date, the first of whom, John de Ramesham, was appointed in 1314.

At some time before 1232, the Abbot and Convent of Muchelney were made Patrons of the living and remained so until the Dissolution. From 1538/1542 it passed to Edward, Earl of Hertford, and from 1542 onwards to the Dean and Chapter of Bristol who retain it to this day.

Figure 1: St Martin's interior

Architecture

The church is constructed of blue lias with hamstone dressings. The chancel is 13th century, illustrated by the two lancet windows, cinquefoiled inside, in the north wall, and also by the grouped lancets of the east window, although the latter was apparently altered in the 19th century. The square headed windows in the south wall date from the 15th century. There is an aumbry in the north wall, a door to which was installed in 1996. On the external wall by the priest's door in the chancel is a scratch dial, rather like a sundial but on the wall. This was used apparently by the priest to tell the time of Mass.

The rest of the building is typical of a small parish church of the perpendicular period, dating from the latter half of the 15th century, although much renewed and extended in Victorian times. The Nave was separated from the chancel by a rood screen, the supports for which can still be seen on each side of the chancel arch. The Rood, or Cross or Crucifix, was positioned on the centre top of the screen and access to it was by the spiral staircase now hidden behind the pulpit.

There is also a squint (hagioscope) cut through the wall, now hidden behind the pulpit. This was usually made to enable a priest at a side altar to follow the main Mass in the chancel. The purpose for which it was intended at Fivehead remains a mystery, but it was obviously for someone unseen to follow the service. A piscina (a stone basin, usually set into the wall, in which the priest used to rinse the chalice and paten) in the south wall of the south aisle indicates the presence of an altar in former days.

The tower is of two stages with battlements, single crocketed pinnacles and diagonal stepped buttresses. Almost the whole of the west face is taken up by the large window which is transomed with panel tracery below, and dates from early 16th century. The windows and bell openings above are filled with typical Somerset tracery of quatrefoils with shields in the centre.

There was a major restoration of the church in 1864 when the south aisle was extended westwards and a new porch added. The barrel roof which probably dates from the 15th century was replastered and the big box pews replaced with the pine ones seen today. The gallery which extended over the Nave at the west end was also removed.

In 1908, the top stage of the church tower was in such a perilous state that a public appeal was launched to raise £1,250 needed to restore it (see photograph).

Figure 2: St Martin's Church Tower before restoration

The Font

The font is Norman, attributed by the Royal Commission on Historical Monuments to the second half of the 12th century and likely to have come from the earlier building. It is circular in shape, lead-lined, with a row of saltire crosses around the top and typical cable moulding around the base. The cover dates from early 20th century.

Figure 3: St Martin's Font

Communion Plate

Fivehead has a silver communion cup which is typical of many in the West Country. There is an identical one at Swell. The paten, or cover, has a spool foot with button base inscribed with the date 1573 and it can be inverted to stand on the altar.

Figure 4: Communion cup and paten.

The Protestant communion cup, post 1525, served a dual purpose. It offered an immediate visual contrast to the Popish chalice with its shallow bowl, straight stem with central knop and concave foot, and it also gave the increased capacity necessary with the restoration of the cup to the laity in 1548.

Towards the end of the 18th century fewer communion cups were produced and the term chalice came back into common usage as pre-reformation designs were copied with the Anglo-Catholic revival of worship. This has continued to the present day. Fivehead has a 20th century chalice made in 1967 by Wippell of Exeter. A silver pyx (a small box in which the Blessed Sacrament is carried to the sick) was donated in 1997.

Memorials

The most noteworthy memorial in the church is a palimpsest brass to Jane Seymour, died 1565, which is mounted on a board on the wall of the south aisle. Jane, daughter of Sir John Walshe of Cathanger, married Sir Edward Seymour, eldest surviving son of the attainted Duke of Somerset, the Lord Protector of England, executed in 1552. The brass was missing for several years but apparently pieces were recovered from a pond in the village early in the 20th century. The shield above the brass shows the arms of Seymour of Wolfhall, Wiltshire.

The reverse shows the figure to be made up of three sections, at the top a section cut transversely from the centre of a

Figure 5: Palimpsest brass to Jane Seymour

large figure of a man's breast. The lower part shows two biblical figures, architecturally framed. To the right is a marginal inscription in Spanish "QUE FINO VIERNES" (who died on Friday) being part of a large 14th century brass of Flemish origin made for a Spanish grave. The lower part shows part of an incomplete inscription to a priest, Gilbertus Thornbern, who died 1428.

At the west end of the Nave are three floor slabs:

1. At the top the Arms of Elyott impaling Wyndham. The inscription below being of Edmund Elyott Esq of Cathanger, died 1725, and also his wife, Beata Elyott, daughter of Sir Charles Wyndham of Orchard Wyndham, died 1749. "She was no less conspicuous for her Benevolence and Charity, than for her Antient (sic) Descent".

2. Here lyes the body of Carolina Wyndham daughter of Sr Edmond Wyndham of Kentsford in the County of Somersett who dyed the 4th of June 1721 in the 87th year of her age.

A very worn slab with inscription round the edges "Here lyeth the bodies of Hugh Pyne of Cathanger Esquier Counseller at Law and (illegible) Bella his wife and were buried in the Yeares of our Lord God 1618 and 1628". The slab is damaged round the edges and not easy to read.

Stained Glass

The glass in the east window depicts Christ in Majesty with the Virgin Mary below and the four Evangelists on either side. This probably dates from the end of the 19th century and was given in memory of William Norman, 1788/1855, born in Fivehead and at one time churchwarden.

On either side on the window reveals are two canvas paintings; on the left, St Catherine of Alexandria, patron saint of Swell Church, and, on the right side, St Martin. The paintings appear to date from early 20th century.

The adjacent window in the chancel contains 14th and 15th century pieces of glass. In the tracery there are delicate floral designs in yellow stain and at the top of the main lights borders of crownwork and various quarries containing similar motifs. According to Canon Woodforde's "Stained Glass in Somerset

1250-1830" fragments include pieces with a pattern not found elsewhere in Somerset.

The south aisle east window illustrates the biblical quotation "Who can find a virtuous women (Proverbs 31:10) and was given by the Matterson family in memory of their mother, Jessie de Mowbray Matterson, died 1930. It was made by Mayer & Co of Munich and designed by AJ Daniells, a free lance designer.

In the central window of the South aisle are two rather fragmentary heraldic shields dating from early 16th century:
1. England and France quarterly surrounded by the Garter
Royal Arms and
2. Gules on a chevron argent a lion rampant sable crowned or, for Brooke, impaling Gules on a chevron or three lions rampant sable, for Cobham.

They are believed to have come from Cathanger and to have been part of a series illustrating the ancestry of Joan Brooke who married John Walshe of Cathanger and was the mother of Jane Walshe of the adjacent brass.

Furnishings

The present altar was given in 1912 in memory of Robert de Mowbray Matterson. The prayer desk was also given in memory of another member of the Matterson family, WA Key Matterson, churchwarden for 30 years, in 1953. The lectern was given in memory of Francis and Rhoda Richardson in 1892. The carved oak screen separating the nave from the tower was erected in 1953.

The free-standing chamber organ appears to date from the mid 19th century. It was installed in 1937 by private subscription. The electric blower was donated by Mrs V Bartlett in 1965.

The oldest Bible in the church has an inscription of 1720 but is believed to be older. The print is in Gothic black lettering and it is bound on thick wooden boards and covered with tooled leather although damaged. The binding has brass protective corners front and back and a lozenge shaped medallion in the centre, all having an embossed foliate decoration. There are remains of brass clasps which would have held the bible closed.

On the front of the bible at the top in Roman capitals is the name FIFEHEAD and below the medallion CATHANGER. Similarly, on the back, STOWEY and MOORETON. Inside the front cover inscribed by hand in ink is written "Arthur Young hys

book (1720). The following was written on the fly leaf at the end of this book:
"Arthur Young was living at Fivehead at the time of John Norman who died there in 1720, as shown by an old deed in my possession, by which Mary, wife of John Norman, sold or let some of her land to him. This book came into the possession of my grandfather, William Norman, and after his death to me, Father of John Frederick Norman.
Compton Norman, 5 January 1878. Restored to Fivehead Church 5 April 1910. Compton Norman"
The bible has recently been treated and restored by the Conservation Officer at the Somerset Records Office.

The Bells

There are six bells, inscribed and dated as follows:

No 1. Inscribed ATTENDITE POPULE (Pay attention people)
A + D + G James Rigbye Vicar 1909
It is 74 cm in diameter and was cast by Llewellins & James Ltd, Bristol in 1909

No 2. Inscribed Sancte Petre ora pro nobis (St Peter pray for us)
It is 74 cm in diameter

No 3. Inscribed SANCTE IOHANNES ORA PRO NOBIS
(St John pray for us)
J RIGBYE VICAR, R DE MATTERSON, H HARCOMBE (CHURCHWARDENS)
It is 81 cm in diameter & was recast in 1909 by Llewellins & James, Bristol

No 4. Inscribed ROBART:COZENS, JOHN DERHAM (CHURCHWARDENS)
CAST BY THOMAS BAYLEY BRIDGEWATER 1765
It is 89 cm in diameter

No 5. Inscribed GAVDE VIRGO MATER XRI
(Rejoice Virgin Mother of Christ)
J RIGBYE VICAR, R DE MATTERSON,
H HARCOMBE (CHURCHWARDENS)
It is 97 cm in diameter and was recast in 1909 by Llewellins & James

No 6. Inscribed ME RESONARE IUBENT PIETAS MORS ATQUE VOLUPTAS (They make me ring out for faith, death and joy)
WILLIAM BAKER ROBERT COZENS (CHURCHWARDENS)
1773 CAST BY THO: BAYLEY BRIDGWATER
It is 107 cm in diameter

Figure 6: St Martins Church 1845 before the Victorian restoration

A note on Mediaeval Church Life

The church before the Reformation was probably the only place big enough for people to congregate. The chancel was the Holy Sanctuary and the responsibility of the priest but the Nave was used for all sorts of activities.

The church was very much the centre of village life. The people were highly superstitious and believed in sin, redemption and the saving of souls. There would not have been the "good taste" of today's church interior; mediaeval churches were colourful places with walls brightly painted and murals used to illustrate the bible stories to an illiterate people

There were no seats inside therefore plenty of space. Disputes and agreements and even manorial matters would be resolved on the church premises. On weekdays, in fine weather, the north, unconsecrated, side of the churchyard would be used. In bad weather, all would congregate in porch and nave.

Except for the chancel, the general maintenance of the church was the responsibility of the parish and was under the control of the churchwardens, a venerable office dating back to the 13th century. Early churchwarden's accounts demonstrate the methods used to raise money needed for maintenance and repair. The yearly festivals were celebrated in the churchyard and one of the most popular was the Church Ale, a festival of sports, dancing and merrymaking together with the drinking of good strong ale provided by the churchwardens who were empowered to raise the money for the brewing thereof, hence the mention later of a church house where this would take place.

The advent of Puritanism in 1603 was supposed to put a stop to all this but it probably continued for some time afterwards.

St Martin's today

After nearly 1000 years existence, what changes are we seeing today?

Some years ago, the Victorian furnishings were removed from the chancel and several pews from the back of the church giving room there for refreshments to be served after services. This did not meet with the approval of many parishioners but churches have had to adapt over the years to meet changing circumstances and ideas.

Our services are being revised constantly, sometimes not always, some think, for the better. There are many new and lovely hymns for us to sing so the musical tradition continues. With the advance of modern technology, PCC minutes, once laboriously written out, are now typed or stored on computer. Suitable hymns for the next Sunday service can now be produced at the press of a button. Is the time rapidly approaching when sermons can be produced in the same way on the Internet?

With fewer clergy, the days of one vicar per parish have long gone. Fivehead is part of a United Benefice with Curry Rivel & Swell and we are fortunate not to have more parishes included. Clergy diaries are full and, where once the vicar visited everyone, many lay people are now involved in pastoral work. We are fortunate to have two lay readers for the benefice, John Heaton and Margaret Smith.

Modern technology cannot solve all problems it seems. The new baptism service involving immersing babies in ancient stone fonts recently caused a problem in Curry Rivel as a suitable plug to fit the drain hole could not be found and the water had nearly drained away by the time that part of the ceremony was reached! It was a rather long service as they had to fill it up again!

However some things never change and the bells still ring out on Sundays as they will to celebrate 2000 years of Christianity. The present bell ringers are Joyce Male, Fred Hollard, Arthur Burge and Maurice Daly. They belong to the Crewkerne Branch of the Bath & Wells Association of Bellringers. They need volunteers, however, to train for this ancient custom to continue.

FIVEHEAD BAPTIST CHURCH

Introduction

Most places in England had Puritan ministers in the time of Oliver Cromwell, and when nearly two thousand of these were ejected after the Restoration of King Charles II most towns and villages had small congregations of non-conformists. Both Fivehead and Isle Abbots had congregations and received new vicars in 1661 to 1662, but in 1669 non-conformists were meeting in the house of Nathaniel Barnard in Fivehead, and their "teachers" were John Baker, George Pierce and John Bush, the ejected ministers from Curry Mallet, North Curry and Langport, and Thomas Marshall, the minister of the Ilminster non-conformists.

In the Return to the Bishop, the vicar estimated the number of those attending the "conventicle" as 200 indicating that people came in from neighbouring villages. Non-conformists then usually described themselves as Presbyterians, but they might be Independents (Congregationalists) or Anabaptists, and often the congregations included all three.

It would then seem that the Protestant cause underwent a decline, as no place of worship for Protestants dissenting from the Church of England was registered in either Fivehead or Isle of Abbots in 1689, when the Toleration Act was passed.

The Toleration Act of 1689 allowed freedom of worship to Protestants dissenting from the Church of England, on condition that they registered their place of worship either at Quarter Sessions or with the Bishop; that they did not worship behind locked doors and that their minister could sign 36 of the 39 Articles.

In 1698, however, the house of Robert Smith in Fivehead was certified as a Dissenters Place of Worship, and in 1715 the house of Robert Smith in Swell. The list of certificates does not make it clear whether Robert Smith had moved to Swell, or was registering a house in Swell where he preached.

We lose sight of Fivehead non-conformists in 1715, unless they walked to North Curry, until John Wesley came riding up from Taunton on Thursday September 3rd 1778 and stopped to preach in the great hall at Cathanger "to a very serious congregation", before he rode on to South Petherton. He came again on Friday 2nd September 1785 on his way from Wellington to Ditcheat and stopped "in an ancient venerable building oddly called Cathanger" where he says "Having a stupid people to deal with I spoke exceeding plain, and I think many of them, even Somersetshire farmers, felt as well as heard". It is just possible that Robert Sweet was in that congregation and with him the story of Fivehead Baptists starts again in 1820.

Figure 7: Fivehead Baptist Church

Origin of the Fivehead Baptist Church

In 1820 Robert Sweet was working as a ploughman for Mr Corpe the Parish Clerk of Fivehead, whose youngest son, Joshua then twenty-one, tried to take a rise out of the old man.

"Didn't see thee in church on Sunday, Robert" said Joshua.

"No Master Joshua, I be Methodist" replied Robert.

"But surely your parish church is the place to worship God" returned Joshua.

There then followed a lengthy reply from Robert as to his beliefs the upshot of which convinced Joshua Corpe to accompany old Robert to Methodist meetings in a hayloft at North Curry. Continuing his Bible study after Robert Sweet's death, Joshua Corpe became convinced that it was a Christian's duty to be baptised, not as an infant but as a believer, and not by sprinkling but by immersion. In 1828 he was baptised and became a member of the newly constituted Baptist Church at North Curry against his parents objections.

Joshua Corpe found himself a wife among the Baptists of North Curry and settled at Stoke St Gregory. After twenty-five years he returned to Fivehead to take over the old family home. Cottage meetings followed, and a staunch friendship developed with William Stodgell, who had also married a wife from North Curry Baptist Church. Every Sunday these four met for prayer and Bible study in the farmhouse kitchen walking afterwards to North Curry to attend two services.

Eventually Joshua felt there was a need to reach their neighbours with the message of the gospel and after inviting people to a service in his kitchen one Sunday evening went and fetched a preacher from Taunton. Sunday by Sunday Joshua drove into Taunton and returned with a preacher and the congregation grew until the preacher had to stand beside the open window with half his audience being outside on the lawn. As the winter approached they moved across to the barn.

About that time Joshua Corpe's eldest son, who had prospered in business, purchased a plot of land adjoining his fathers barn, and offered it to the congregation as a building site. A building fund was started and was well supported. Some who could not afford to give money gave help in carting stone. Joshua Corpe printed and sold for twopence a four-page folder of verse appealing for gifts.

In 1866 the building was ready and the local paper reported the opening. "The new Baptist Chapel was opened on Thursday and a large number of persons assembled to celebrate the event. Service was held in the chapel in the morning, when the Rev S Newman of Salisbury preached a sermon. A capital dinner was provided in a large marquee which had been erected in a field behind the chapel. The marquee was nicely decorated with floral devices and in the centre of the tent there was a curious device composed of teazles and flowers forming a graceful as well as novel feature. The local name of this collection is The Harvest Handful or The King of all Teazles. After dinner a public meeting was held".

For the first two years the new chapel relied on supply-preachers until the spring of 1868 when on March 8th 1868 the chapel was constituted as an independent Baptist Church. The first pastor was Benjamin Osler who also managed to be Pastor of North Curry and Isle Abbots at the same time. Founding members were Joshua and Anne Corpe, William and Caroline Stodgell, Susan Corpe, Christopher and Richard Hallet, William Bicknell and three members of the Marsh family.

Early church meetings were concerned mainly with applications for baptism and church membership. Collections were taken occasionally for incidental expenses. In August 1874, to help Fivehead finances, Mr Osler bought the orchard adjoining the Manse for £100 " Until such time as friends can re-buy it".

At first the membership figures of North Curry and Fivehead are shown as one total in the statistics of the Western Baptist Association, but from 1874 North Curry is shown alone, while Fivehead is linked with Isle Abbots. In that year Mr Osler accepted a call to the Pastorate of Barnsley Baptist Church.

The early years

Mr John Burnham of Pastors College was preaching in the villages around Wellington in the summer of 1874, so he was invited to preach also at Fivehead, and in October he was offered the pastorate of Isle Abbots and Fivehead, for a stipend of £75 and a house, which he accepted.

"Three very happy years", wrote Mr Burnham, " were spent in Somerset, but the strain of constant service in two places with little help and less ministerial fellowship thoroughly broke my health and obliged me to retire".

Mr Osler came to the help of the church again, partly by writing from Barnsley, and also by coming to preside over a very important church meeting. In his letter Mr Osler recommended to the church The Rev John Compston, his predecessor at Barnsley. The son of a Lancashire Congregational minister, John Compston was the author of several books and a musician of some distinction. In Yorkshire Mr Compston had stood on the platform beside Samuel Plimsoll in his campaign against "coffin ships".

On Mr Osler's suggestion he preached at Fivehead and in May 1878 Mr Osler presided at a church meeting which agreed to offer the pastorate to Mr Compston. John Compston accepted and moved to Fivehead at the end of July 1878.

The new ministry commenced with great activity and membership of the combined church of Fivehead and Isle Abbots grew steadily. In June 1880 membership stood at 76, with 92 Sunday School pupils and 10 teachers at Fivehead, with 38 and 4 at Isle Abbots.

The manse was burnt down in October 1881, but was rebuilt and inhabited again before the next summer at a total cost of about £400.

When Joshua Corpe died in 1884 a church meeting ordered a special resolution to be entered upon the records of the church. "That this church desires to place upon the record the feelings of love and esteem cherished for the memory of its oldest member and first deacon, brother Joshua Corpe. It cannot be forgotten that our departed brother was, under God, the founder of this church. His love for souls, his zeal for truth, and his concern for the cause and Kingdom of our Lord Jesus Christ being honoured of God in the realisation of his strong desire for the establishment of a Baptist Church, and the erection of a chapel and Sunday School in Fivehead.

The church was kept aware of world affairs, and when the news came that Khartoum had fallen, the Church sent a memorial to the Right Hon WE Gladstone, First Lord of the Treasury.

"The members of the United Baptist Church of Fivehead and Isle Abbots in the County of Somerset, while deploring the unfortunate death of General Gordon, would earnestly deprecate the prolonging of hostilities in the Soudan for purposes of revenge or conquest, or military prestige, or for breaking the power of the Mahdi. They urgently implore Her Majesty's Government not to persist in the purpose of sending our troops to Khartoum, but to content themselves with safeguarding the national boundaries of Egypt proper, leaving the people to possess their own land, to cleave to the Mahdi if they choose, and to manage their own affairs".

Mr Compston had buried his eldest surviving son, Milton, a student Baptist minister, in Fivehead churchyard, a few years previously, and in April 1887 Mrs Compston was laid beside her son. It was a loss from which the Pastor never recovered. He informed the deacons that he would be resigning as from January 1888. Mr Compston died not long afterwards in London on Easter Sunday 1889.

The Rev B Osler again came to help the church, this time with a month's ministry and the recommendation that they should hear the Rev Edward Francis of Bridport. At the end of March 1888 Mr Francis was invited to become the minister of the joint church and in June he commenced his ministry.

About that time Mr Joseph Corpe gave the church a piece of land adjoining Fivehead Chapel, and the deacons recommended the building of stables on it, and the raising of a special fund for the purpose.

Membership again increased and in 1892 reached 92. Church meetings during this time were concerned mainly with the appointment and reports of visitors to candidates for baptism and membership, and with repairs and improvement. Dry rot in the floor of the schoolroom at Fivehead necessitated the draining of the site as well as complete replacement of the floor.

In 1893 old William Stodgell, co-founder of the Church with Joshua Corpe died, and his funeral showed the great respect in which he was held. His wife survived him only as far as the New Year, and the Church's Resolution of Appreciation was recorded in the Church Book. Mr Osler preached the funeral sermon.

At the end of 1894 Mr Francis resigned and almost five months passed before a new Pastor, the Rev Edward S Hadler was appointed. Mr Hadler began his ministry in the early summer of 1895 and in October the church agreed to the formation of a Young People's Christian Endeavour Society. When Mr Hadler left to take up the Pastorate of Burton Stogursey, sixty members signed a letter of thanks and good wishes, and presented him with a purse. His preaching, his work with young people, and his visitation of the sick had been particularly appreciated.

In 1899 Rev G A James became the next pastor but did not remain long resigning in 1903 because of his wife's serious illness.

1900's

In 1904 James T Schofield became the next pastor settling in July. The minister preached at Isle Abbots and Fivehead alternate Sunday mornings, at Isle Abbots on Sunday afternoon, and at Fivehead in the evening. The new pastor's preaching and visiting were valued highly and each year concluded with a small grant supplementary to his stipend coupled with an expression of appreciation.

In 1908 Isle Abbots Baptist Church celebrated its centenary with up to 250 people attending.

In December 1910 a great gale blew down the manse chimney stacks, which fell through the roof, and necessitated urgent repairs at a cost of £68. A grant towards the expense was made from the fund called "The Chapel Case" but members subscribed nearly £40.

At the end of 1911 Mr Schofield consulted the Church, asking if members thought a change of pastor would be in the best interest of the Church. Of 58 ballot papers sent out, 52 were returned, unanimously asking the pastor to stay. There had been a slight storm, when a member, a local preacher, had been accused of attending horse races, betting, and attending a prize-fight. His offence proved to be a case of "only once" and he was exhorted to "be not conformed to this world".

Friction in Fivehead Sunday School in 1912 was followed in 1913 by a difference of opinion between the two congregations about the sharing of expenses. In 1914 an unfortunate incident nearly dissolved the partnership of Fivehead and Isle Abbots. A rather small but quite regular church meeting at Fivehead did not re-elect the senior deacon, who had actually been censured by the Church for his personal attacks on a previous minister. Another deacon went around collecting signatures for a letter of sympathy which appeared to invalidate the election. Mr Schofield called another church meeting at Fivehead which upheld the action of this deacon. So serious did this seem to the Pastor, that, fully supported by the Isle Abbots members and by two of the Fivehead deacons, he felt he could no longer continue his ministry at Fivehead and must seek another pastorate. In the meantime he continued his ministry at Isle Abbots. An attempted reconciliation broke down resulting in the members at Fivehead to begin looking for a new minister. The members at Isle Abbots held that the members in the two chapels formed one church; those at Fivehead maintained that there were two churches which for convenience shared a pastor.

In the autumn of 1915 Mr Schofield accepted the pastorate of the Baptist Church at Rye in Sussex. On December 1st the members from both villages met, under the chairmanship of the Rev AW Holden of Hatch Beauchamp, to agree about the financial obligations they were prepared to accept, and to invite a new minister for the pastorate. After a disappointment in January, the two congregations agreed in the spring to invite the Rev Joseph Day of Devizes, and he accepted the pastorate of the two churches, on which he entered in the summer of 1916.

Mr Day's ministry made possible a gradual healing of the wounds, though at first the relations of the two churches were rather distant and formal. A Manse Renovation Fund was started and the Isle Abbots Church made a contribution. Jubilee services at Fivehead were proposed for 1917 but in the stress of the war no celebration was arranged.

Mr Day had been invited to be Pastor for five years and was re-invited unanimously for another five, and then later "without fixing a time limit". However in March 1927 Mr Day explained to the two churches that as he was forbidden to cycle he was finding the distances too much for him to carry on his work among them, and he had therefore thought it right to accept the invitation he had received from the Baptist Church at Faringdon, Berks. It was with sincere regret that the two churches accepted their Pastor's resignation.

It took the churches nine months to find their next minister, but in January 1928, the Rev SR Ward came from Wythall, Birmingham.

Electric light was installed in Fivehead Chapel, the schoolroom and in the manse in 1938, the lights being given by the present families or in memory of past members. The old lamps were subsequently sold to the Women's Institute. The installation at Isle Abbots was made in 1942-3.

In July 1946 Mr Ward died having been pastor to the two churches for eighteen and a half years. The minutes of the church referred to him as "a well loved and respected Pastor".

For two years Albert Adams and Frank Millar presided at their respective church meetings and arranged for preachers throughout that time. In March 1948 the Rev W Jenkins of Pembroke preached at both churches, and without asking him to preach again, the members sent him an unanimous invitation to the pastorate, on which Mr Jenkins entered in July. The manse was then renovated inside and out, and Fivehead Chapel also in 1951. In 1956 Mr Jenkins left having accepted the call to the Pastorate of Roch Chapel in Haverfordwest.

During the next two years Miss Ethel Humphry occupied and took care of the manse, becoming acting secretary and presided at some of the church meetings. Then in August 1958 the Rev E

Emlyn Thomas took up the pastorate, but his four years at Fivehead were punctuated with much illness, and in October 1962 he felt that he must resign.

In the autumn of 1962 the Rev CLB Plumb was teaching in Ilminster, and the Rev H Pewtress, the Area Superintendent, suggested that the two churches might consider asking him to combine his teaching with the pastorate. He preached in both chapels, was invited and accepted, starting his ministry in January 1963. During his time both chapels had electric heating installed along with electric blowing of the organ at Isle Abbots. In the summer of 1965 Mr Plumb accepted another teaching post in Cheshire and resigned the pastorate.

In July 1966 the Rev HE Nutkins came from Hatch Beauchamp to be pastor to the two churches. At once he began preparations for the centenary of the formation of Fivehead Baptist Church, for which a most attractive renovation was completed. The church was full for the re-opening service on December 17th 1967. The Centenary Celebration was held on April 25th 1968. In January 1969 the Trusteeship for the Church and Manse was passed to the Baptist Union Corporation. A joint pastorate with Hatch Beauchamp and Fivehead Baptist Church, linking five churches together, was proposed in March 1972, but was turned down by Hatch Beauchamp. Rev HE Nutkins then retired in October 1973.

During the rest of the seventies little happened to the church although in February 1975 the Manse was exchanged for a house in Silver Street, into which a new minister, Rev E Hough, moved. In March 1978 Rev E Hough retired to Canada and a Mr and Mrs M Jarrett moved into the Manse temporarily. Then in October 1979 Rev B Johnson began his ministry; at this time the membership at Fivehead stood at eight with the minister also acting as secretary.

In March 1984 there was unfortunately a fire in the church's toilet block and after an inspection by a Fire Officer it was found there was a need for a fire escape for the upstairs rooms, otherwise they could not be used. Funds were raised and in January 1988 a fire escape was in place. Around this time all the wood in the church, including the roof, was treated. A new wooden floor was also fitted to the schoolroom.

In recent years there have been good relations with St Martins Church. In March 1985 Mrs R Reading of the Baptist Church began a joint children's work with Mrs M Barrett of the anglican church. A Youth Club was also given permission to use the schoolroom on Saturdays. In September 1995 a joint Harvest Service with St Martins Church was held.

Reg Yarde, the church treasurer, died in June 1992; he had attended the church all of his life. Not long after, in July 1992, Rev B Johnson left and was replaced by Rev L Caldecourt in January 1994 and a notable event occurred in April 1994 when the first baptismal service was held for 31 years. In December 1997 Rev L Caldecourt completed his ministry and in October 1998 Rev S Perry arrived to continue the long life of the church.

Note on source. The principal source has been "A Short History of the Baptist Churches at Isle Abbots and Fivehead" by W MacDonald Wigfield MA.

LANGFORD MANOR

Langford Manor situated on the east side of Fivehead, beside the lane leading to Swell, derives its name from "long ford". In 1255, it was known as La Langeforde.

The house is built in the shape of a double E, although the original design was probably T-shaped, and is constructed of local greystone. A little to the east of it is the Stewards or Dairy house. It is not known who built the house, but it is thought likely that the house is of two distinct dates. The oldest part, the east wing and the great hall, is considered to be pre-Elizabethan, whilst the west wing and porches are middle 17th century. The chief features are the Ham stone porches and fireplaces, mullioned windows, vertical panelling of pre-Elizabethan date, mostly in elm, and the Tudor staircase of oak and elm, built round an elm newel, which rises to the top of the house in easy bends of five steps each. The gables have crow-foot terminals.

Figure 8. Langford Manor (sketched by Bill Mead)

The first mention of the manor, at the time known as Langford Fyfehed, occurs in 1251, when Sybilla de Gundevill quit-claimed to Sabina del Ortiary, the lady of Curry Rivel, all her rights in Chory and Langford.

The next owner, whose name was adopted from the manor, was Roger de Langforde in 1309. Thence it passed to the following: John de Langforde in 1327, who was the sole local taxpayer; Sir Thomas de Langforde in 1372, who sold it to Francis de Scoland; in 1411 it belonged to Francis de Scoland's widow, Ernestine. In the reign of Henry VI it belonged to Thomas Beauchamp and Aleanor, his wife.

A major change came about in 1518 when Sir John Speke, who married the heiress of Sir Thomas Beauchamp, conveyed by legal process the manor with 130 acres of land and 52 acres of meadow, to pass on his decease to the Cathedral of Exeter. This was in return for "an honest and sad priest to sing and say mass weekly and daily as after he shall be disposed in the new chapel of St George made and founded by me with the said Cathedral of Exeter. The Dean and Chapter retained the Manor of Langford for over 300 years.

During the ownership of the Dean and Chapter of Exeter, the different tenants included Sir John Clifton, of Barrington. His first lease was granted for a period of 21 years at 13s 4d per annum. John and Walter Seymour, sons of Edmund Seymour of Cathanger, subsequently held the manor and farm for the length of their natural lives. In 1625, the sons gave place to the daughters, a lease of the manor and farm being granted to Arthur Champernowne and Christopher Blackhall for the lives of Margaret, Mary and Ann Seymour.

In 1649 the Seymours gained freehold of the manor when all Chapters where annulled by Cromwell, but they then quickly sold it to Nathaniel Barnard, the son of Nathaniel Barnard of Downside, Shepton Mallet. This family was of some note in the county and inter-married with the neighbouring family of Strode. The cousin of the Nathaniel in question, Joan, becoming the wife of William Strode, of Barrington Court.

However in 1661 the King and the Chapters came into their own again and Barnard was compelled to take out a lease for the estate, of which he thought he was the freeholder. After the Barnard's the next tenant was Colonel Henry Brett. The Brett's held the Manor of Whitestaunton for many generations. The Colonel was Churchwarden of Fivehead in 1720.

In 1726 a lease of Langford Manor was granted to Sir Abraham Elton, who had bought the Manor of Whitestaunton from Colonel Brett. Sir Abraham was succeeded by his son in 1732. In 1765, Francis Wright, gentleman, of Creech St Michael, came for 21 years, followed by William Richardson, of Durston, who held it in trust for his son, Francis. He in due course acquired a considerable amount of land in addition to this manor. He was succeeded by his son, Henry Richardson, a well known sportsman, who kept a pack of hounds at Langford.

In 1860 the estates of the Dean and Chapter were transferred to the Ecclesiastical Commissioners. It then became the freehold and residence in 1904 of the Matterson family, first of Mrs Jessie de Mowbray Matterson and then from 1930 WA Matterson, Esq, JP. A restoration of the house was carried out by the Matterson family. Mr W Arthur Key Matterson lived in the manor until he died in 1953.

In 1953 the house was bought by a Mr Harris and sold the same afternoon to a Mr and Mrs Walker who lived there until 1957. The manor was then bought by Dr Muir who lived there until 1962. The house then stood empty for several years until it was bought by Mr and Mrs Whiffin.

In the 1970's considerable restoration and alterations were carried out. The manor also changed hands in the 1970's being bought by Mr and Mrs Charles Levison.

In the 1980's the manor was divided into two dwellings. One side was occupied by Mr Andrew Garlick and the other by Madeline and Peter Willis from 1982 to 1985. Jenny and John Gilbert then lived in one part from 1983 to 1987.

The house was restored to one dwelling and Charles and Anna McMiran lived there from 1987 to 1992. In 1992 the present owners Peter and Fiona Willcox moved into the manor and have run it as a Bed and Breakfast establishment from April 1996 to November 1998.

Reference: Langford Manor, Fivehead, by WA Key Matterson.

CATHANGER

Cathanger, the name of a manor house and manor, lies in the parish of Fivehead on the south side of the main road from Taunton to Langport. Its name means "the slope frequented by wild cats", although there is another possibility that it was derived from the old English word Hangra, meaning a wooded hillside.

Cathanger itself is a very old place. In the time of Edward the Confessor, nearly a thousand years ago, Cathanger was in the possession of Wadel, a noble Saxon. After the coming of William the Conqueror, Wadel was dispossessed and the manor was granted to the nearby Muchelney Abbey. It is mentioned in the Domesday Book when it belonged to the Abbey of Muchelney.

There then follows a gap of over a century in the descent of the estate by which time Muchelney Abbey had relinquished Cathanger and taken over Fivehead manor and church. The next known owner of Cathanger was Robert de Osberville who held the estate until 1193. However he had supported Prince John while Richard I was abroad as an Austrian prisoner awaiting ransom. Hence, on the King's return, Osberville forfeited the estate for treason.

Figure 9: Cathanger (Sketched by Bill Mead)

In 1197 ownership was with William de Wrotham which then passed to his nephew, Richard son of Richard de Wrotham. Richard died childless in 1236 and his heirs were apparently his four sisters. One of these, variously called Emma or Margaret, had married Geoffrey de Scoland and died before her brother, leaving a son, Geoffrey de Scoland, aged 24 in 1250. When the Wrotham inheritance was divided up between the four heirs, Cathanger manor was granted to Geoffrey.

Geoffrey died in 1288 leaving a widow, Benedicta, and son Richard, aged 30. The house was then held with a garden, wood, 169 arable acres, 15 acres of meadow and pasture, and 32s 4d a year rent from tenants. Richard de Scoland leased Cathanger manor to the Hospital of St John of Jerusalem, but either he was dead by 1290 or there were doubts as to his legitimacy, for in that year the property was seized by Edward I on the grounds that Geoffrey's nephew and heir was a minor. Geoffrey's brother, Franco de Scoland, had died in 1285 leaving a two year old son of the same name. When this son, Franco de Scoland became of age in 1300, he regained the property from Edward I and eventually settled the lands on himself and his wife Alice in 1325.

The property remained within the Franco de Scoland family until in 1428 Thomas Walshe was noted as the owner. By what means the estate passed to the Walshe family is not clear. Some sources indicate that Franco had a daughter, Eleanor, who married Thomas Montague and that it was by this route that the manor was inherited by the Walshes. The estate then passed down through various sons of the Walshe family until in 1507 it was in the hands of John Walshe who through his first marriage transformed the fortunes of the family. He married Joan, daughter of John Brooke, Serjeant at Lawe, Judge of Assize and Chief Steward of Glastonbury Abbey. Evidently the twin influences of grandfather and uncle led her son, John Walshe, to enter the legal profession. This John Walshe grew up to become Chief Justice of the Common Pleas and builder of the earlier parts of Cathanger that can be seen to day.

The rebuilding of the mediaeval house, which was probably completed in 1559 as there is an inscription on the wall of the house which reads "John Walshe Anno Dni 1559 Serjeant at Lawe" was obviously intended to mark his rise in the world. This was quickly followed by an even more important step when his only daughter, Jane, married the second but eldest surviving son of the attainted and executed Duke of Somerset, former protector of England, becoming Lady Jane Seymour, and niece to her more famous namesake who had married Henry VIII.

John Walshe gave his new son-in-law a lease of Berry Pomeroy manor in Devon and this new branch of the Seymour family subsequently seated themselves there. When John

Walshe died on 12th February 1572 all his lands including Cathanger, passed to his ten year old grandson, Edward Seymour.

The next most significant change for Cathanger came when Edward Seymour's eldest son and successor, Sir Edward Seymour of Berry Pomeroy, broke the link between house and family, continuous from 1197, by selling the building to Hugh Pyne, member of a young but increasingly influential family from the neighbouring parish of Curry Mallet. The actual date of the transfer has been lost but lies between 1613 and 1618.

Hugh Pyne, like Walshe before him, was a successful lawyer who put his savings into land. He had two children, Arthur and Cristabel, of which Arthur inherited the property after his father died on 21st November 1628. However Arthur did not enjoy his inheritance for very long before he himself died on 4th April 1639. As he had died childless Cathanger passed to his sister, Cristabel, wife of Edmund Wyndham, eldest son of Sir Thomas of Kentsford.

Cristabel was not only considered to be one of the beauties of England at the time but was also intelligent and observed to be of a stronger character than her husband. It was evidently she who wrung out of Charles I lucrative sinecures in the law for her husband and in 1625 Queen Henrietta Maria chose her to be wet nurse to the infant Prince Charles. In the civil war Edmund and Cristabel inevitably declared for the king but after the success of Cromwell suffered the total ruination of his estates through heavy fines. It would appear that he managed to hold onto Cathanger however as Edmund later claimed that Cathanger was only held in trust to pay Christabel's widowed sister-in-law, Grace, a jointure of £300 a year following her wedding to Cressy Tasburgh.

Following the death of Sir Edmund the descent of the house becomes rather vague. Edmund's eldest son, Sir Hugh Wyndham had died before his father in 1671 and, although he left children, Cathanger seems to have been left to a younger son of Edmund and Cristabel, Sir Charles Wyndham who was an MP for Southampton and St Ives. On his death in 1707 he left everything to his wife Jane. By the time she died in 1720 only one of her ten sons and four of her seven daughters were still alive. At this time the house at Cathanger was occupied by Henry Huddy, a yeoman, and subsequently by Sir Charles's unmarried sister, Caroline Wyndham, who died there on 4th June 1721, aged 87.

Cathanger Farm, as it was called in the 18th century, then passed into the hands of one of Sir Charles Wyndham's daughters, Beata, wife of Edmund Elyott, page to the Duke of York, the future James II. She died childless in 1749 and is buried in Fivehead Church. However her complex will bedevilled the descent of the house for over 70 years. She left her property to her sister Frances White, who died childless in 1754, and then in trust for her cousin and nephew, Thomas Elyott. His father had been the brother of Beata's husband and his grandmother, Elizabeth Elyott had been the daughter of Sir Edmund and Cristabel Wyndham. The problem was that the bequest to him was entailed and thus should have descended to his heirs. Despite this, having moved to Italy and having no children, he sold Cathanger to Joseph Bullen for £2,600 in 1792, subject to Beata's will. Elyott died in about 1807 and Bullen by 1795 moved into the house. In 1817 Robert Uttermare Bullen, under whom the house had been occupied by William Selway, 1814-15, assigned Cathanger to the Rev Charles Phillott and Francis Dorothy his wife, in trust for the wife's father, Francis Pender, Vice Admiral of the White.

The tenant during the years 1781-94 was a farmer, John Stone, who was converted to the new Methodism. On the 12th January 1785 the house of Cathanger Farm was licensed for nonconformist worship, Stone himself being one of the seven applicants. John Wesley preached in the great hall of Cathanger on at least two occasions, 3rd September 1778 and 2nd September 1785.

Wadham Wyndham of Salisbury, survivor of a distant branch of the Wyndham family discovered evidence of the entailed estate which, following numerous deaths and legacies, should have come to him. On the basis of this evidence he started a law suit against the unfortunate Phillott family then in residence, and in 1824 surprisingly won it. However he had to pay heavy compensation to the Phillotts in the form of an annuity of £200 a year for the rest of their lives, but having obtained possession, Wadham leased the farm in 1825 to John Harcombe at a rent of £500. The Harcombes, who moved in from Middlezoy, occupied the house for just over a century.

John Harcombe died on 25th February 1834 and the farm passed to his sons, Joshua and James. In 1851 Joshua was in sole possession of the farm and 267 acres, employing 19 labourers. Joshua died in about 1890 and was followed at

Cathanger by his son Henry, who worked the farm until its sale by the Wyndham's descendants in 1927.

The purchaser in 1927 was Mr RH Anderson, a Scotsman, who bought the house and 93 acres of land, and brought his wife and two daughters down from the north. He restored the old house and in 1931 described its situation as follows; "Cathanger faces a southerly prospect of broad acres well timbered with evergreen, oak, beech, mulberry and elm. It forms an ideal grassland farm. Water has been piped to all fields and a distinctive system of free-range poultry farming is worked". A number of his farming improvements owed much to his skill as an inventor and he added a tennis court in 1938. The house with its 93 acres was sold in 1952.

From 1958 to 1985 Cathanger was the home of Mr and Mrs PGW Clarke but since then has changed hands several times.

The house is L-shaped with the main part, consisting of two storeys and attics, orientated in a N to S direction. The wing to the W leads off the N end. The wing comprising a Great Hall with a large room over it, reached by a spiral staircase, and the Tudor bedroom were added by John Walshe in 1559. The wing possesses some good examples of hollow chamfered mullions, widespread in Somerset and used throughout the sixteenth century. The door below the staircase is an example of a three-centered arch common in the fifteenth and sixteenth centuries. The bedroom contains a small sixteenth century fireplace and there is a larger example in the Great Hall. The other wing of the house stands on the foundations of a much older building, apparently destroyed by fire and rebuilt around 1720. The drawing room extension was added in 1920.

The gatehouse at the end of the garden was never intended as the main entrance to the house, nor for defence, but is a sixteenth century folly. On the garden side are two shell topped niches, probably copied from Montacute. The blue lias stone has been arranged to form a decorative part of the structure, alternating with layers of freestone.

Beyond the gatehouse is a pigeon loft containing twelve hundred holes, a hole for every acre of the estate at the time it was built, and one of the largest in the country.

OLD BUILDINGS IN FIVEHEAD

General information

Fivehead contains several buildings of historical importance, with the Church of St Martin's probably being the oldest. The church is a 13th century Grade I listed building. The presence of a Norman Font and a well raised graveyard suggest the present church occupies the site of an earlier church; the site may have been the focus of Saxon occupation.

The main focus of mediaeval settlement was around the church with the surviving older domestic buildings occupying small irregular plots nearby. About half of these face on to a rectangular open space to the east of the church.

From either side of the church the lanes run parallel up the hill to the main road. Towards the north end of these lanes near the main road there were several cottages occupying narrow plots parallel to the lanes; of these Briar Cottage and Mount Pleasant still remain. This development probably represents squatting from the 16th century onwards and reflects the growing importance of the main road to the north of the village. Slight earthworks in fields between the village and the main road represent the sites of 19th century lime kilns.

Source: Mediaeval villages in South East Somerset by Ann Ellison.

Listed buildings

The listed buildings for the village are divided into two groups, those which are Places of Worship and those which are Secular.
Places of Worship.
Grade I: St Martin's Church, Fivehead, and St Catherine's, Swell.
Grade II: Baptist Church, Fivehead.
Secular Buildings.
Grade I: Swell Court Farmhouse.
Grade II: Cathanger Manor, its Gateway and Gatehouse, a barn in farmyard to the north of the Gatehouse, and a barn in farmyard to the south of the Gatehouse; Langford Manor; Park Gate Cottage; Red Post House and forecourt railings; The Old Forge; Tudor Cottage and forecourt wall; Mount Pleasant; Briar Cottage; Spring Grove; Stowey Farmhouse and Squirrelsmead Cottage.

Village Hall

Prior to 1971 the Village Hall was the Fivehead Parish Elementary School. Although there had been a National school in the village for some years before, the present building was erected in 1874 to accommodate 110 children (mixed sexes); in 1906 average attendance was recorded as 71, falling to 60 by 1914.

The building is a typical of similar period village schools, being single-storey, stone-built from the local lias limestone with two principal rooms. The school bell can still be seen in the small bell-tower.

Figure 10: Fivehead Village Hall circa 1939 when it was still a school

When the Somerset Education Authority announced the closure of the school in 1971, a small group of villagers under the chairmanship of Commander John Hoover USN (ret) set up a Trust Deed to buy the building for the use of the village as a Village Hall. Work was done to adapt the school premises to suit the needs of a Village Hall by adding cloakroom facilities, kitchen and entrance foyer. In compliance with Grade II listing, this work was done without altering the building facade. More recently, further work has been done to bring the hall into line with Environmental Health Legislation.

Red Post House

This house, located at the top of Butcher's Hill, and built of the local stone Blue Lias, was erected in 1780; its name indicates that it was beside a turning point for the postal service. On the top road we now know as the A378, adjacent to the house, was an island of three fir trees surrounded by box hedge. Coaches would have turned around here.

Figure 11: Red Post House (sketched by Bill Mead)

The house contains many original features but has also had an interesting history during the 20th Century. In the early past the extension on the road side was used as the local post office.

During World War II, 1939 - 45, Mr John Claude Elmar bought the house and with his mother and local help ran a boy's school until his death in 1967. The school was named Aethelmar. Mr Elmar was known as "Skip" and being a polio victim was confined to a wheelchair, although this did not prevent him from organising many outdoor activities. He also started a local club for boys aged 8 to 14 years, named the Boy Pioneers; activities included tracking, cricket, football, camping and swimming in the river.

Higher Langford Farm

This lovely old farmhouse, built in 1690, was a working farm until the 1980's when the surrounding land was sold by Somerset County Council and Langford Close was built on the land.

The house is basically constructed of Blue Lias and many original features have been restored by the present owners. In the living room, as well as a large Inglenook, the original pump and sink for drawing water from the well are to be found; lining the Inglenook are herringbone tiles so placed to minimise damage from the heat of the fire. In the lounge is a large Inglenook with a large bread oven. Above this fireplace is an oak beam with adze marks in it for plastering.

In one of the chimneys, during restoration, a letter from a daughter of a previous resident was found. The letter dated

1886 is from a girl to her mother and father. The letter was sent from Shebbear School in Devon and gives quite an insight of life at the school and of the era. Teazels were also found in the roof indicating that this must have been an important crop produced by the farm. It is believed that the room at the east end was a village shop at one time.

Foxhound Farm

This farm situated on the main road in upper Fivehead was a thriving Public House until 1974. The place had been a Public House certainly since 1859 when James Witcombe was licensee. In 1861 Charles Harvard took over and in 1883 John Gridley was licensee until 1889. In 1897 Harry Maddick became licensee and was still there in 1919. From 1935 to 1939 Mrs Mary Dare nee Maddick was recorded as the licensee.

The land now owned by the Foxhound Farm had many owners and occupiers on the 1840 Tithe Map. Some of the fields were owned by Wadham Wyndham of Cathanger but leased to Joshua Harcombe. The farm was a grower of teazels at the height of the teazel trade.

In 1937 Brutons Beers bought the property but by 1964 Bass Charrington was the advertising brewery. In 1972 the brewery sold the property to Mr and Mrs Maddick who continued running it as a pub until 1974. It then became a popular Bed and Breakfast en route to Cornwall.

Figure 12: The Meet at the Foxhound Public House

In recent years the farm has changed hands several times. In July 1976 the Maddicks sold to Mr and Mrs Eade, who bred horses during their time there. It was then sold to Mr and Mrs W HN Judd in September 1979; they ran a small holding breeding pigs. In October 1983 Geoff and Judith Skinner bought the farm and as well as breeding pigs, specialised in goats, marketing their own goats milk ice cream. The present owners, Philip Hacon and Mary Simmons, bought the property in May 1988. They run it as a successful sheep farm and breed specialist English Goats. They have also developed a nature walk which is open to the general public at certain times of the year.

Coins

Located at the top of Ganges Hill, next to the main road, this house was a bakery during the 1930's and also a general store during World War II. A bread oven is still visible in the house but the steps to the shop door were covered during rebuilding of the corner in 1997. One interesting feature on the outside of the house is a bench mark for the use of the Ordnance Survey.

Mrs Kathleen Maitland, who lived in the house from 1978 to 1998, remembers when she had just moved in during the winter of 1978/79 that the snow was waist high outside.

Tudor Cottage

Tudor Cottage is a thatched property situated on the eastern side of the parish church and it abuts onto the war memorial land. It could just have been built during the reign of Queen Elizabeth I (she died in 1603), for its beginnings originate from the turn of the 15th century. Tudor Cottage and its forecourt wall are Grade II listed. This means that the owners are not allowed to alter its features without permission of the Council.

The present name "Tudor Cottage" is of a relatively recent date, being known as this, according to the records of the deeds, only since 1926. Prior to this date it was known as "Farm House and Little Plot" or just as "Fivehead Farm".

The thatched bonnet hood over the front door leads to a flagstone cross-passage which divides the cottage into two halves, indicating that it was built to the old mediaeval plan. This has been confirmed by a recent visit of a carpenter to the property. Oak was more in use for houses built in mediaeval times.

On the right hand side as one looks at the cottage from the road, the downstairs room, now used as a dining room, would in its early days have been the kitchen with a huge inglenook fireplace. The inglenook was modernised at some stage and replaced with a 19th century carved decoration, similar to that often seen in churches. Behind and to the right of the fireplace is a "type 2" curing chamber. It has a rounded wall and, when in use, the ceiling here would have been partially open to the stack above to allow the smoke to escape. There are two ledges at waist height and across these there would have been bars on which the meat to be smoked would have been placed. Behind here the front part of the bread oven exists; but the rest has been blocked up, perhaps when the Baptist Church was built.

On the western side of the cross-passage, (the room on the left as seen from the road), is the living room. From the earliest times it will have been used as such, although in the 1600's it would have been called the "parlour" or "hall". This room was always built on a higher level than the kitchen so that there was no danger of kitchen waste flowing into the main living quarters.

Figure 13: Tudor Cottage

The eastern side, at the rear, with its many beams of elm, is now the kitchen; but, until about 1984, it was a study and, prior to that, a morning room. Earlier still, it consisted of at least two rooms which would have provided service rooms for the old kitchen; a pantry perhaps and a laundry, making it a sort of early type utility area. It is of interest that the stud wall, between the former kitchen and pantry, has one panel of exposed wattle and daub.

On the west side of the house is a small window with a peaked head and a chamfered stone frame. This is very old; certainly early 1600s, or even late 1500s. It has the character of a stair window, but is set too low to function as such.

In the courtyard outside is a covered well. A lady, who used to be a live-in maid at Tudor Cottage for twelve years during the 1930s and 1940s, has recently paid a visit to look at the place where she used to work. Among her memories is that of a man who came once a week to the kitchen to pump up water from the well to a tank in the loft so that the upstairs had a supply of water for the bathroom. A rope hung down from the tank, so that the height of the rope would indicate how much water was left in the tank.

The date "1789" is on a stone in the wall near the back door and on the front gate post are the initials "W.C." followed by the date "1871".

It has not been easy to establish who lived at Tudor Cottage in its earliest years. It is thought that in these times it was rented out. Prior to 1864 it was owned by the Yeo family. There is some evidence to show that a John Corpe rented the property from 1782 and lived here with his wife and ten children; his wife, named Mary, lived here until she died aged one hundred. Tudor Cottage was probably rented by one of John Corpe's sons, Joshua, who lived in the property from 1855 to 1880. According to the deeds, which are in the possession of the present owners, Joshua's son, Joseph Corpe, who was a grocer in Windsor, bought the property outright from the Yeo family in 1864. The property remained in the possession of the Corpe family until 1915. Joshua Corpe is listed in Kelly's Directory of 1861 as being a "farmer and butter factor". He also founded Fivehead Baptist Church. It is said that the village Pound, now at the bottom of Butchers Hill, was originally on the site of the church. Baptist services were held in one of the rooms at the back of Tudor Cottage until the church was built.

Around the time of the end of the 1939-45 war sewing classes were held in Tudor Cottage run by a surgeon's wife. One of the ladies who lives in the village can remember these and, as the girls sewed, passages from Pilgrim's Progress were read to them.

Much of the above account is based on a survey of Tudor Cottage undertaken by Commander EHD Williams, with additional information provided by Mr J Dallimore and Mrs L Hall. Other information has been provided by Mrs H Blake, Mrs C Birch (nee Corpe) and Mrs M Saint. To all these people, very many thanks.

The Old Forge

A rubble walled house with thatched roof and upper windows in eyebrows. The house was originally of a two room plan of 1600 origin with later additions in the 17th and 20th centuries.

The central doorway is in a massive chamfered wooden architrave with four-centred head and planked door with strapped hinges.

The room on the left of the door has a fireplace from the side of which the original spiral stairs probably rose. There is an oven on the left of the fireplace.

The central room was originally unheated but the central brick stack rising from eaves level assumes an added fireplace, now removed.

Figure 14: The Old Forge (sketched by Bill Mead)

The further rooms to the right were added in the 17th century and also the rear extension including the stairs, the roof over this extending in a continuous downward slope to a lower eaves level. In the wall over the stairs is a stone ovolo moulded single light window.

The further addition to the east was added in 1932 and what was the old smithy was converted into a self-contained annexe in the 1980's (?). Features of interest include chamfered ceiling beams, fireplaces with large wooden bressumers (supporting beams) and panelling.

The Crown Inn

The Crown Inn is located opposite the church. The old part of the building is 13th century, being the same date as the church. It may have originally been a church house.

However it has been run as an Inn for the past 200 years. The current licensees (1998) are Jan and Billy Cousins.

Houses built of local stone

Figure 15: The building of Swell Wood House 1938

Many of the older properties in the village, both large and small, have been built of blue lias, a local stone; white lias was also used. One of the last houses to be built with white lias is Swell Wood House situated, as the name suggests, on the edge of Swell Wood.

Swell Wood House was built in 1938 as was Weavers Lawn, situated half way up Butchers Hill. Weavers Lawn is built of both blue and white lias. The local builders, Maude - Roxbys, would probably have built more but with the out break of World War II in 1939 all house building had to stop. This also coincided with the closure of the local quarry.

Fivehead Village Bakery

One of the longest surviving bakeries was situated in the centre of the village next to the present Post Office. A Mr William Hillard is listed as shopkeeper and baker in 1861, and the same family continued to run the shop and bakery at least until 1939.

Thence the bakery was run by Mr Hembrow until 1953 when Mr Peter Maisey took over; his wife Hilary ran the shop. At this time food rationing was still in place. There was a major fire in September 1959 at the bakery, but customers' supplies were kept up with the help of Peter's father who ran the family bakery at Othery.

Figure 16: Maisey's Shop

In 1961 the shop also took over Post Office duties which included sorting the local mail for Isle Abbots, Isle Brewers, as well as for Fivehead at 5 o'clock in the morning. Hilary Maisey continued running the shop and Post Office, with the help of two assistants, until 1976, when the shop was sold and separated from the bakery. Peter Maisey continued baking bread, having as many as five delivery rounds, until March 1988 when he sold the business to Mr Keeley. Mr Keeley continued for approximately three years and then sold to Mr Priddle. The bakery finally closed down in February 1992.

The premises are now occupied as offices for a local consultant civil engineer, a Mr Barry Baker, whilst the shop and

Post Office continue as a thriving business now run by Jean and Lynn Griffiths.

EVENTS AND LIFE IN FIVEHEAD AND SWELL

Fivehead memories

Ella Louch was born at Bridge Cottage, Fivehead, Sept 7th 1921 and died in Jan 1998, having lived all her life in Fivehead. She attended the village school when the head mistress was Miss Blanche Titterton, with the junior mistress being Ethel May Thomas, daughter of Charles Thomas. At the age of 11 Ella had to go by taxi or bus to Curry Rivel School as Fivehead was only a junior school by then.

Ella described in great detail "Club Day" held each year, the last Thursday in May, by the Fivehead Male Friendly Society. Another special day in the school's calendar was Empire Day celebrated on May 24th. She did not have regular pocket money but would be given money at Christmas, on birthdays, or for a Sunday School outing. As the children grew older they were able to earn extra coppers by running errands, picking blackberries or by helping in the teazel fields.

Ella remembers a company of Girl Guides being formed around 1932/33. Meetings were held weekly in the Lambert Hut but ceased when the leaders moved away. When the Second World War started in 1939 everything changed; there were evacuees, rationing, planes overhead and long weary years, but many new friendships were formed.

In her earlier years Ella remembers travelling by wagonette and horses driven by Mrs Harriet Fox and son Jack. Mrs Fox also brought back work from the factories including that of shirt making, collars, pinafores and gloving, which was worked on by hand and machine. Fresh milk and butter was collected from the farms before laws came into force banning direct sales.

Another celebration that Ella talked about was the Baptist Chapel's Anniversary held on Whit Sunday; new outfits would be worn including a new hat. Whit Monday was a day for a lovely tea followed by an evening service.

Mrs Ivy Duke was born 24th September 1900 and died February 1992, aged 91 years. Ivy's family the Hillards were involved in the Fivehead Bakery for nearly 100 years, a William

Hillard being listed in Kelly's Directory as shopkeeper and baker in 1861. Entries continue with different members of the family until 1939 when Robert William Hillard was listed as grocer.

Ivy attended Fivehead Village School until she was 14 years old, knowing Head Masters Charles Thomas and John Beake. Having left school she also became involved in the bakery. She remembered the bread wagons delivering bread during the winter to Isle Brewers in the flood waters, which came over the horses back. The bread would be thrown up to the bedroom windows and by The Mill the cart had to be turned around. "When we got to The Mill we had to shunt back to turn the cart into the straight. As soon as the horse felt the wheel touch the bank he would move away. We never had to touch the reins, he would always lead us through".

During Ivy's time at school half a day each week was devoted to gardening. The grassed area at the Village Hall was a garden tended by the children, with the boys being encouraged to grow vegetables whilst the girls grew flowers. In her adult years she was also involved in the work that was brought to the village from the factories, such as Van Heusens. This mostly involved collar work but sometimes whole shirts were produced. Ivy also made many pairs of gloves, handmade stitched ones and those lined with sheepskin. They would have to cycle into Taunton to collect the gloves. In 1935 one could also travel into Taunton by horse and cart for 6d; return fare being 9d.

In 1931 Kelly's Directory lists Francis Fox as a carrier weekly on a Saturday and Miss Talbot midweek. Ivy also remembered when Coins was a shop at the top of Ganges Hill and when the Old Forge was a working forge.

From an interview conducted by Paul Northcott and Margaret Hole in 1991.

The Post Office in Fivehead

Although a London Mail existed as long ago as Tudor Times, it was in 1665, by decree of Oliver Cromwell, that a nationwide postal service was established. Then in 1740, John Palmer of Bath put the first Mail Coach on the road, and this in a strange way affected the tiny, sleepy, remote village of Fivehead!

In 1765 the Prime Minister, William Pitt the Elder, came to Curry Rivel to claim the estate he had inherited from William Pynsent at Burton. He agreed to a coaching road being cut through his land. At that time the existing road turned south at the Bell Hotel, Curry Rivel, and proceeded to Exeter via Hambridge, Barrington and Ilminster. The proposed road would join the Bell Hotel to the Taunton turnpike at Red Post House, Fivehead, and it was completed in the late 18th Century.

Figure 17: Delivery of the mail at Red Post House

In 1840 Rowland Hill started the Penny Post and the quantity of mail increased dramatically. Post Offices were quickly established, the first being at 5 Angel Row. By 1901 it had moved to Red Post House and the Postmistress, Miss Beatrice Milton, was presented in 1926 with an engraved gold watch for long, cheerful service. Mrs Sidney Salway next took over and the post office was run from Vale View, Butchers Hill, then for a time from Dinhams Cottage, Fivehead by a Mr Herbert Adams. In the war years, from 1939 to 1945, Mr Charles Dunkling took charge from his house "Cambourne" near the Foxhounds Inn. After the war a Mr & Mrs Smith ran the post office from Brakelands on the main road and when they moved to Millers Orchard its home was a wooden shed on the allotments opposite the Lambert Hut. When this land was acquired to build the Glebe, the post office moved finally to its present site, the village shop, under Mr & Mrs Peter Maisey. Mail was delivered in bulk and sorted for distribution at Isle Abbots, Isle Brewers, Upper and Lower Fivehead. By then it was important enough to have two postal persons, Mr Bert Adams and Miss D Keitch.

The village shop was sold in 1976 to Mr and Mrs Fookes-Bane and in 1979 to Mr and Mrs Williamson. In 1981 Mr and

Mrs Elberton bought it and stayed until 1982 when Mr and Mrs Mills took over. In 1987 Bill and Agnes Robertson bought the shop and stayed until June 1997 when Jean and Lynn Griffiths took over.

Doctors and nurses who have attended residents of Fivehead

At the turn of the century Dr Richard Vereker was the local doctor holding surgeries at his home in Curry Rivel. He would do his house calls by pony and trap in the early days, progressing to a motorbike and sidecar as time went on.

Dr John Glover took over from Dr Vereker but was tragically killed in a road accident driving to a patient late at night. Dr Muir became the local doctor during his residence at Langford Manor (1957 - 1962). Dr Butterfield then took over from Dr Muir, but as the work load increased a group practise was formed in Langport. Today Fivehead residents can register at a surgery at North Curry or at the Langport practise.

Figure 18: Nurse Dora MacDonald

The District Nurse at the turn of the century was Dora MacDonald who would do her rounds by bicycle covering Isle

Brewers, Isle Abbots as well as Fivehead; the photograph is dated January, 1923. Nurse E Firth took over from Nurse MacDonald, also serving many years. Nurse E Slack took over from Nurse Firth.

Village school life

The following extracts are taken from the Head Teachers Log Book found in the church vestry covering the years 1875 to 1891. The entries, picked at random, demonstrate the difficulties encountered at the time of poor attendance for a variety of reasons, of illnesses no longer encountered today and the poverty of some families unheard of in these days of the welfare state.

May 6th 1875. Charles Thomas, CM, received the Log Book and the Portfolio from the Rev RW Lambert, Vicar.

May 7th 1875. Attendance of girls small on account of heavy rain.

July 6th. School closed for the afternoon, the Anniversay of the Fivehead Female Friendly Society, causing non-attendance of scholars.

July 16th. School closed for the day to permit the teachers to attend the Royal Agriculture Show at Taunton.

October 1st. Attendance has been very small. Potato digging has begun, scholars absent to pick them up.

May 25th 1876. The members of the Male Friendly Society held their annual meeting on this day, in consequence of which, the school was closed for the day.

April 7th 1879. William Sparks sent three of his children to school this afternoon but they were so dirty and their heads full of lice that the master sent them home for the mother to clean them before they could be admitted.

April 16th. Miss M Gange visited this afternoon and instructed the upper girls in knitting, she also supplied some with wool.

June 11th 1880. The weather has been fine these last few days and the older boys have been more absent than usual. The girls have not attended quite so well as so much collar work was brought from Taunton that the mothers keep home little ones not 7 years old to help finish in time. Total attendance 56 with 84 on the registers.

June 18th. Three boys, Fredk Hooper, Edwd Hooper & George Bostock played truant yesterday afternoon, the last named boy is found to have done it on several occasions and to have

tutored the others to do the same. Their parents have punished them and they will be kept in school after time to do extra lessons.
December 19th 1881. The master has found out that Mary Salway has been telling lies for the last two weeks by saying that her young brother is very ill "with a breaking out all over his face" while at the same time he was in the fields scaring the birds. She was told to say so by her mother.

Figure 19: School photograph; Mrs Male far right

March 20th 1882. Alice Scott is very ill, there seems to have been a gathering in her head, and now it discharges through her ears. She has been in such pain, but is now easier. Her parents think she had better not attend school, or will not be able to for some time. She has always been weakly in mind as well as body.
May 23rd 1882. Lilly Smith has been absent for some time and her mother cannot spare her as she has such a little family to look to besides dairy work, so her name is struck off the registers. She was ill last birthday.
November 15th 1882. The weather is very stormy still, some of the little ones get quite wet by the time they are here as they have nothing extra to protect themselves with.
February 12th 1883. We have had rain falling the whole of the day, and only a few children living near were able to attend school, the roads in some places being covered with water

several inches deep, also in several houses which drove the families upstairs.
February 23rd 1883. Thomas Squire, Mary Squire, Sarah Squire and Alice Salway were called to go home before school closed as the father of the Squires was drowned in the moor, he having overloaded his boat which sank beneath him, while his boy managed to lay hold of and save himself by the head of a withy tree which was just above the water's edge, the water being from 7 to 8 feet deep.
December 19th 1883. Several children are kept away this week most probably anticipating the school holidays and, as usual, making a fortnight's holiday into a month.
July 4th 1884. Infant Class; "E Male is a promising teacher, she has taken much pains with the Infant Class and with decidedly satisfactory results" (E Male was the mother of the late Tom Male, verger of the church).
November 11th 1884. Louisa Stodgell is seriously ill with diptheria, has been for some days but is now got worse.
November 13th 1884. The Hare Hounds are out today and some living near the place of rest (Foxhound) are allowed to remain from school, as usual, to see them as they pass.
November 17th 1884. Louisa Stodgell died Saturday night after severe suffering, her throat seemed to have swollen so much as to prevent her breathing. Age 9 years 11 months.
Several scholars are still ill while a number who are at school often start coughing so much as to interrupt the classes, it being whooping cough, causes so much noise.
March 2nd 1885. Alice Salway and Rosa Webb have not been much lately, the excuse the parents send is that their shoes are bad.
July 10th 1885. Edwin John Salway was punished for taking part of another boy' dinner. The master gave him a stripe on each hand and stood him out in front of the class with a card at his back marked "Thief" until 4 o'clock. It seemed to affect him much, and it is hoped to have the desired effect of preventing him doing so again. One or two dinners have been lost lately but no one could be found to have taken them.
November 9th 1885. Several scholars are absenting themselves this week; blackberry, potatoes and apple picking form the principal employment just now and, as the Officer has not hunted up lately, the parents keep them at home when they like.
March 16th 1888. Eight infants have been away from school the

whole of this week, most of the absent ones are ailing with one complaint or another, but most have scabbed heads and faces, some with boils on their bodies. One boy could not sit for three days but, living near, he came to school and stood.

April 11th 1888. The poorer class of children are often sent to the copse and fields to gather primroses for sale; 30 primroses and some ivy leaves in a bunch for ½ penny.

September 26th 1888. Blackberry picking has commenced in this neighbourhood; the vendors get 1 penny per lb.

November 7th 1888. Thomas Edmonds, Mabel Mullins and M Webber are home with no shoes fit to wear in the rainy weather.

July 24th 1889. A little of the Harvest has begun such as the cutting of oats and next week some of the farmers will begin with the wheat as well as teasel cutting which usually lasts six weeks.

August 1st 1889. A good number of scholars are absent this week as the busy time is come. By the consent of the Managers the School was closed for the Harvest vacation, viz, four weeks.

September 9th 1889. School re-opened after five weeks holiday, the managers having consented to an extra week as the gleaning and teazel cutting was not quite over, and now only about half have returned for blackberry picking has begun and is likely to affect attendance for about six weeks.

September 14th 1891. This school is now free for all scholars from 3 to 15 years of age.

September 28th 1891. A large number of the Upper Standard are absent, some keeping pigs for the farmers, others picking blackberries. Free education is not appreciated by a goodly number of the parents as they think a "screw" will be put on them if they do not send their children more regularly to school; they would rather pay and be freer.

December 14th 1891. Some of the boys and girls are off at times to pick ivy leaves and sell them at 3d per dozen bunches. One boy may earn as much as 2 shillings a day which is very tempting to keep them from school. Free education does not benefit the scholar so far, in fact it seems worse for the child, and also vexing for the teacher!

December 22nd 1891. A large number of children are away with influenza colds.

The logbook finishes at December 24th with following remark: The children assembled this morning were sent home for their Christmas Holidays as the Master has influenza and is unable to get out.

In the summer of 1891 there were 97 children on the registers. Where did they put them all?

ACCOUNT OF MONEY SPENT ON THE BUS SHELTER

As there was money left over from the Coronation Celebrations, Mr Male, Mr Trebbeck and Mr Hooper decided to make collections from the village to add to the amount to build a bus shelter.

FIVEHEAD CORONATION COMMITTEE
BUS SHELDER 1954

RECEIPTS			PAYMENTS		
Collections			Materials - sand, cement, chippings, timber, tiles, nails etc.		
T. Hale	£ 14.11.0		W. Potter & Sons Ltd	£ 33.0.0	
T. Hooper	5.12.6		H. Hoskings Ltd	4.19.11	37.19.11
E. Trebbeck	2.18.0	23.1.6			
			Oak Board & Inscription per Caswell & Grant		2.7.6
Donations					
Western National	3.3.0		Stamp Duty on Agreement per Somerset C.C.		10.0
Hutchings & Cornelius	3.3.0	6.6.0			
Surplus on Coronation Celebration Funds		10.6.1			
		39.13.7			
Deficiency donation, W. Hollinrake		1.3.10			
		£ 40:17:5			£ 40:17:5d

W. HOLLINRAKE
(Hon. Treasurer)

Figure 20: Building of the bus shelter 1954 with monies left from the Coronation celebrations of 1953 (Erected by Bill Saint).

Empire Day May 24th
(Late 1920s early 1930s)

The children in the village school spent weeks preparing for Empire Day, learning poems and songs about our colonies and land overseas, and how important they were to us. On the afternoon of Empire Day, the children with their teachers went in procession through the village to Langford Manor. The Matterson family were entertained with the result of the children's efforts and afterwards everyone was given a large Bath bun well spiced and sugared by RW Hillard, the village baker. The children were also given a bar of chocolate.

Queen's visit to Somerset June 2nd 1966

It is recorded in the Somerset County Gazette, dated Friday June 3rd 1966, that the Queen and Prince Philip visited Curry Mallet and stopped to meet the oldest Duchy Tenant in the area. This lady Mrs Caroline Taylor, then aged 91 years, had been born and married in Fivehead, later moving to Isle Abbotts. She had 21 children, and her oldest grandchild, Mr Frank Goodwin, still lives in Fivehead.

From Curry Mallet the Royal Party travelled through Fivehead and the Brownies lined up outside the Garage and Red Post House to cheer them on.

SOCIETIES AND CLUBS

Male Friendly Society

The Male Friendly Society was formed on Dec 11th 1865 to help its members in cases of ill health, as families were not able to afford medical treatment; it also helped the widows on the death of the member.

The highlight of the year was Club Day held on the last Thursday in May. On the Wednesday the Fun Fair arrived; in the 1920s it was Richard Townsend & Sons from Weymouth who bought all their equipment on huge trailers towed by powerful fairground engines. This was set up in Doctors Ground, a field kindly lent for the occasion by Arthur Troutt of Manor Farm. This is the field behind the old vicarage, and the entrance was by way of the lane where the phone box now stands. As the field adjoined the Lambert Hut, it was convenient for serving teas.

The evening before the President's chair was prepared in readiness for him to preside over the meal next day. The chair was very high backed and covered in golden chain (Laburnum) and red peonies as well as other greenery and flowers. The village was also decorated, and the brass birds cleaned for the top of the poles; Fivehead's was a dove to represent the one sent by Noah from the Ark and these were handed down from father to son.

The women were busy boiling hams and making gooseberry tarts from the first gooseberries of the season which were picked for club day and were eaten with rich cream from local farms.

On the day at about 6 o'clock in the late 1920s, Walter Stodgell, who was deaf and dumb, would be seen accompanied by several children raising the flag on the church tower and soon after the bells would start to peal. Club members and families dressed in their best started to arrive from surrounding villages except Curry Rivel who had their own group. One family arrived in a large taxi from Over Stratton. The Treasurer/Secretary at that time was Edward Gridley, who then lived at the old vicarage opposite the church. The President was Francis Mead of Langport; he owned a large grocery store there and would arrive in a horse drawn carriage. He was followed in later years as President by William Key Matterson who lived at Langford Manor.

At 10 o'clock a procession would form. The men wore a rosette on their hats and a button hole of a fresh flower. The pole was carried over their shoulders with blue ribbons flowing from the top under the brass dove. The club banner was carried by William Priddle and later by his son. It was royal blue with tassels and an inscription worked on it saying "Bear one another burdens". It was heavy and constantly mended by Mrs Grace Gridley, mother of the club secretary. When mending was no longer possible it was then taken to Taunton Museum, and another banner purchased. This was not as good as the first, but when the club ended it was hung in St Martins' Church, were it still is. The men then marched behind the band followed by many women and children usually up Butchers Hill, along the main road and down Ganges Hill, calling at Manor Farm, before ending at the church for the 11 o'clock service. As this meant passing the Crown Inn, several stewards were appointed to keep order and see that no one took a wrong turn into the Crown. If they did a fine was imposed.

The first hymn would always be "All people at on Earth do Dwell", and the sermon contained a mention of the number of people who had not been seen in church since the previous club day. After church the programme continued with the meal. In the early years a cooked meal had been provided by Alfred Dinham of Tanyard Farm, and this was delivered by horse drawn carriage. Cider was a popular drink and barrels were provided; they would arrive the evening before and were tapped in readiness. Speeches continued until about 3 o'clock in the afternoon when they then processed to Langford Manor and were there entertained by a band. The children all had a day off school and one of their favourite treats was the ginger breads sold at the fair, where most people stayed to enjoy themselves until midnight. The club ceased to function just after the 1939 war began.

The Fivehead Fellowship Club

Some 30 years after the disbanding of the Friendly Society a few of the former members, together with others, formed a Committee to launch a new club for villagers over the age of 60, of both sexes. The inaugural meeting took place on 9th December 1969 with Mr S Miller in the Chair. Mr Jasper was the Treasurer and Mrs M Rowe was the Secretary (Mrs Rowe is the only surviving founder member of the club). Other Committee members were Mrs I Duke, Mrs A Trout, Mr W Trunks and Mrs H Male (some of the reminiscences of Mrs Duke are featured elsewhere in this volume).

It was decided that the club should meet on the first Tuesday of the month from 7 to 9pm in the Lambert Hut, and that Mr Percy Luxton should be asked to stand as President of the Club, which he agreed to do. The first meeting was on 6th February, 1970.

At the second meeting of the Committee, on 22nd January, 1970, a list of Rules of the Club were drawn up. These Rules remain substantially unchanged to the present day, except that the qualifying age has now been reduced to 55 years. The Rules defined the aim of the club as being "to provide entertainment, pleasure and fellowship for the members".

The Club got off to a very good start with 20 members at the first meeting and new members joining at every meeting, the total rising quickly to more than 40.

At the Committee meeting on 11th May, 1970, Mr S Miller, in the Chair, reported that Mrs Matterson, of Langford Manor, had expressed a wish to attend a meeting, and the Secretary was asked to write to invite her to attend the June meeting.

By August 1970, Mr Jasper had asked to be relieved of the post of Treasurer and Mrs Duke was appointed to take over as Treasurer. She continued in this post until the end of 1988.

During this first year of the Club's life various entertainment's, outings and parties were arranged. One of the early speakers, in October 1970, was Mr Harry Driffield (now, in his turn, a member of the Club), who talked about the Hydrographic Office.

The Club thrived during the 70's, it would appear, although the minute books from 1974 to 1982 are missing.

By 1982, Mr Bert Adams was the Chairman, and Miss Marshall was the Secretary, Mrs Rowe having resigned in February 1982. Mr Adams also held the post of President, and in 1983 asked to stand down as President since he felt it was wrong to hold both offices; as a result Mr Berkley Johnson was elected President and Mr Adams remained as Chairman. This situation continued until the death of Mr Adams in 1990. At the Annual General Meeting following it was decided that it was unnecessary to have both President and Chairman, and Mr Johnson was confirmed as Chairman.

The 18th Annual General Meeting on 1st December, 1987, was the last to be held in the Lambert Hut. By this time membership had fallen to 20 members. Miss Marshall resigned the Secretaryship in 1988 and it is worth quoting part of her Report for the year: "Our meetings have lacked support this year, even though we met at the Village Hall where it was nice and warm. We have had good speakers who were really enjoyed by those who came to the meetings. Our usual Harvest Meeting was not well-supported, we only made £12 - a loss on other years. We held two Bring-and-Buys, the first one raised £12.43p which was enough to pay for the Hall for these meetings, but the second lacked support, but I think we have made enough to cover expenses of rent of the Hall. Not much has been done to help finance our Club; no raffles have taken place which would have paid for milk, tea and biscuits. I am afraid our Club is fading away which is really sad for all who have worked hard to get it going".

This plaintive swansong of Ethel Marshall's marked the low point of the Club's fortunes, since it slowly regained its strength and vigour and now, ten years later, is one of the most active of the village organisations. This has only been possible because the founders started the Club on a sound basis and because of the foresight of people such as Ethel Marshall who recognised the symptoms of decay and sounded the alarm.

Today the Club has a membership of over 50, and provides an ambitious and varied programme of meetings with talented entertainers, and interesting speakers on a wide variety of subjects. There is an annual Theatre Trip in January, outings in May and July and a Lunch Meeting in February. The traditional Christmas Lunch and, for those who wish to go, a visit to St Audries for their Christmas Party, round off the year's entertainments. Club finances are boosted by Raffles, stalls at the May Fair and Christmas Fair in the Village Hall and at Fun Day. There is also a lending library and an occasional produce stall. The Club also sponsors and organises Chairobics Classes under a professional instructor to give the over 55's a means of keeping fit and mobile through gentle exercise; these classes are open to non-members.

Millennium year will be the 30th Anniversary of the Club and the Club can be relied upon to make its contribution to the Village Celebrations and is determined to continue to adapt to the needs and wishes of its members into the next century.

The Lambert Hut

This was an important meeting place for all the village for many years; Miss Lambert, daughter of a former vicar of Fivehead, gave the land for the hut to be built for the service men, known as the "Old Contemptibles", who had returned from the First World War. It was built in 1919 and demolished in 1996.

Figure 21: Nativity Play in the Lambert Hut 1964
(Top row: (left to right) Sarah Weymouth; (Angels) Lynne Saint, Mary Clarke, Karen Saint; Nicholas Paul; Helen Solway; Nigel Daniel), (Middle row: Tim Hodson; (Mary) Gillian Maisey) (Bottom row: George Clarke; Douglas Weymouth; (far right) Miss Paul; Julie Luxton)

On the foundation of the British Legion (now the Royal British Legion) in 1920 the "Old Contemptibles" were incorporated into the Curry Rivel, Drayton and Fivehead Branch of the Legion, making it one of the earliest of the Legion's branches.

Remembrance services were held in the hut where all denominations could meet. This was also an important venue for the Male Friendly Society who would meet here on Club Day to eat lunch following the parade through the village. The Women's' Institute first met in the Lambert Hut in October 1956. Girl Guides also met here for many years.

After the hut was demolished the land was sold and two family houses were built on the site.

Fivehead Playing Field

A sports committee existed in the village and they organised events, etc, to help purchase land for the Playing Field. Land was purchased 1958-1959 and the Playing Field was officially opened on Saturday July 22nd 1961. A summer fete was held annually including a fancy dress parade with the carnival queen riding through the village to the field on a float.

Figure 22: Crowning of the carnival queen 1965 Princess: Gillian Maisey, Queen: Patricia Murphy, Princess: Patricia Salway

In spite of having a playing field the cricket team had to play across the road on Mr Trent's field until Mr Peter Clarke bought a bungalow on Stowey Road and gave the land adjoining the playing field to enable a cricket pitch to be sited there. It was about this time that the pavilion was built. Over the years tennis courts and a children's play area have been added.

The Sports Committee changed to the Playing Field Committee and the Summer Fete eventually became Fun Day where all organisations can take part and anyone can enter the Flower, Craft and Produce Show, and everyone can enjoy the day.

Fivehead Parish Newsletter

This is published bi-monthly by Fivehead Parish Council. All organisations are invited to contribute to the newsletter and every household receives a copy free.

Fivehead and District Women's Institute

The first meeting of Fivehead and District WI was held on October 11th 1956 in the Lambert Hut at Fivehead. There were 43 members present, of which 27 stood for committee. Mrs Walker was elected as the first president. The Fivehead and District WI was then affiliated to the Sedgemoor group under the County Office, Wilton Lodge, Taunton. The first of many teas to come was then served, price twopence, and a Notice Board was donated by Mrs Matterson and a tray by Mrs Dunkling.

At the first Annual General Meeting a resolution was proposed to change the day of the meetings but the motion was defeated. The financial balance at that meeting was Sixteen Pounds and Ten Shillings. At around this time a drama group was formed and was active for many years resulting in some fine performances and many gold stars. Photographs of the drama group are recorded in the WI's scrapbooks.

In 1958 the institute approached the County Librarian with a request for the village to be visited by the Library van rather than just having books being dropped off. This was granted and still takes place today. During the same year Mrs Matterson gave a dozen teaspoons to the institute and WI crested crockery was bought. A wall hanging with the words of Jerusalem was also obtained.

Figure 23: Fivehead Produce Show 1965; Mrs Marjorie Glover (Doctor Glover's wife) is presenting the cup to Mr Pat Cleary (back left: Mr Sid Miller; back right: Mr Douglas Maddick

In 1959 members approached the Parish Council to get place names and litter bins for the top road, the outcome of which proved to be successful. The first WI Produce Show was held in the Lambert Hut the same year. Another activity, that of a choir, was started in 1960 and also continues today. Tea had now increased in price to four pence. A change at this time bought about the Fivehead and District WI joining the Isle Valley Group. For the second WI Produce Show Mrs Leach gave a challenge cup which is still strongly contested.

In 1961 members were urged not to leave the meetings early but this proved difficult to overcome as there were young children to look after when school finished for the day. Mrs Bartlett, then Headmistress of the school, agreed to keep the children until 4pm and Mrs Slade ran a creche for the younger children.

In 1963 a link was formed with Harptree in Saskatchewan, Canada. This resulted in lots of interesting correspondence and visits. Among other notable events of 1963 a green cloth for the Presidents table was presented by the handicraft class and members became involved in compiling a booklet The History of Fivehead, spearheaded by Mrs Leach; this was published in 1964. A proposal was also made to change to evening meetings but this was defeated. The price of tea stayed the same.

In 1965 the village gained a high profile when Westward Television turned up to film an institute meeting; apparently all the best hats were on show! During this year an offer was made to the Parish Council for the WI to maintain the Pound, the small enclosure at the bottom of Butcher's Hill Lane. This was accepted and a lot of hard work went into cleaning it up. WI members still look after it on a monthly basis to keep it going. Mrs Leach gave a stone seat for the Pound and in 1968 a plaque was put up. By 1966 membership had risen to 54 and in the same year the WI made another contribution to the village by having a Village Notice Board put up on the Crown Inn wall.

In 1968 a village meeting was called to decide whether to turn the now redundant school into a village hall which is what eventually happened with the WI being much involved in the change. During 1969 the WI decided to leave the Lambert Hut and held meetings at the Baptist Church, the Crown Inn, the Village School and Cathanger. A permanent move to the Village Hall was made in 1971. Around this time the WI donated staging for the Drama Group along with six trestle tables, two dozen cups and saucers and a large teapot. Mrs Brettel donated a silver inkwell for competitions at the Flower Show; this is still in use for WI members. A tree was planted at St Martins Close to honour the Queen's Silver Jubilee.

In 1975 a Heritage Book was compiled of Fivehead and District. This was entered for a European Architectural Heritage Year Competition and won one of ten gold stars presented to Somerset. A ballot took place in 1977 to change to evening meetings but the result was a stalemate. However it was decided to give the evening meetings a try; they are still held in the evenings. Membership was 53 in 1977 and increased to 61 in 1978. The cost of a cup of tea was now 10 pence. In 1979 at the suggestion of the Parish Council a Fun Day Committee was set up with the WI taking part; they provided a display and teas.

In 1981 The Old Village Chat Show was held and a video produced. It was a full house with Mr Ken Male as compere. Guest speakers were Bert Adams, Ella Loach, Ray Yarde, Tom Male, Arthur Murray and Jack Salway. The video was entitled Fivehead Remembers. The same year a copper beech tree was planted in the playing fields to celebrate Fivehead and District Womens Institute.

In 1982 the link with Harptree was discontinued. A new link was formed in 1983 with Yeelanna, South Australia. Visits where made by Mr & Mrs Proctor in 1992 and a strong fellowship has grown up. In 1985 the WI amalgamated with Fivehead Fun Day to hold a joint flower and produce show in the playing fields. This continues to the present day with the WI also supplying teas. Shrubs were planted in the Pound in memory of two past presidents, Mildred Dodd and Kay Evans. However membership of the WI was now beginning to decline and in 1986 it was down to 36 members.

In 1987 members approached the Parish Council for a speed limit through the village but found that there was a ten year waiting list; in 1998 the speed limits came into force. In 1987 a tree, an acer, was planted in the cemetery to celebrate the Somerset Federation of Womens Institutes 75 years anniversary. 1990 was the last group meeting of the Isle Valley Group and Fivehead transferred to the Taunton Vale Group. The price of a cup of tea at the meetings was now 15 pence. In 1995 the WI members catered for the 50th Anniversary celebrations of Victory in Europe and Victory in Japan events; hard work but enjoyable.

In 1996 a dinner was organised at the Blackbrook Inn, Taunton, to celebrate 40 years of Fivehead and District Womens Institute. A Celebratory Centenary dinner was held in the Village Hall to mark the start of the WI movement, 100 years ago, at Stoney Creek, Ontario. The village church bells were rung in honour of this and members and guests enjoyed an evening of nostalgia. In 1997 a joint venture with the Village Hall Committee to produce a map of the village was completed successfully. In 1998 there were 26 members of Fivehead and District Womens Institute; the price of a cup of tea having reached 20 pence.

Fivehead Girls Club

This club was started in September 1968 and held weekly in the Lambert Hut. A group of mothers, Mrs Clarke, Mrs Maisey, Mrs Smith, Mrs Amor, Mrs Saint and Mrs Scammells, felt there needed to be more activities for girls aged 10 to 15 years and formed a committee. Activities included Netball, Tennis and Drama. The Drama was so successful that four members of the group came first in the Improvised Drama Class for 12 years and under at the Bath Festival in 1969, and two more members came fourth in the Duo Improvised Drama.

Figure 24: Fivehead Girls Club Drama win 1969 (left to right: Jo Clarke; Mary Clarke; Lyn Davis; Clementina Zielenkiewicz; Nicola Stiles)

The club had more than 20 members and was well supported. By March 1970 the committee decided that some of the girls had outgrown the club in its present form and thought that joining forces with the Boy Pioneers to form a Fivehead Youth Club might be a better option. This did happen and in 1971 the Youth Club had at least 45 members of which 10 members were under 15 years and 35 members were over 15 years.

One highlight was when the Youth Club were invited to the Bingham Sports Centre in Nottingham to take part in the finals of "Its a Naycout" on Saturday May 13th 1972. They were led by Mike Wheller, accompanied by Jo Clarke.

Fivehead Playgroup

There are sufficient under 5 year olds to run a Playgroup in the Village Hall two mornings a week. A Mother and Toddler group also meets on another morning.

1st Fivehead Brownies

This was first registered in January 1966 then closed in April 1970. It was re-opened in May 1979 and suspended in May 1987. The present group was re-opened in January 1988 and was still going strong in January 1999.

The Guiders, who are the leaders known as Brown Owl, have been: Mrs Joan Perrin and Mrs E Salway, 1968-1969; Mrs D Broganza, May 1979 to April 1980; Mrs Jane Trundley, October 1980 to May 1987; Mrs Wendy Cutts, January 1988 to September 1990; Mrs Sheila Land, 20th September to the present day.

The group usually has an assistant Guider known as Tawny Owl. These have been: Miss I Duke; Mrs Wendy Cutts; Mrs Lyn Creed; Mrs Sheila Land, January 1988 to September 1990; Mrs Wendy Cutts, September 1990 to March 1992; Mrs Pam Randall, September 1991 to March 1993.

Brownies is for girls aged 7 to 10 years. The unit is called the Pack and is divided into Sixes. The girl in charge of the Six is called the Sixer, with the next one being called the Seconder.

Figure 25: Fivehead Brownies taking their promise
Back row, left to right: Mrs Joan Perrin (Brown Owl); Sue Pester; Karin Saint; Lynne Saint; Cynthia Priddle; Naomi Barrett (County Commissioner); Eileen Jones (Divisional Commander); Jean Dabinett (Tawny Owl))
Front row, left to right: Gillian Maisey; Helen Salway; Linda Harris; Angela Murphy; Carole Priddle; Margaret Bawler; Suzanne Waites.

Pre-enrolment takes about 4 to 6 weeks. Each Brownie must understand the motto "Lend a hand", the law, a Brownie thinks of others before herself and does a good turn everyday, and finally the Promise "I promise that I will do my best to love my God, serve my Queen and Country, to help other people and to keep the Brownie Guide Law". The girls then take their promise round the toadstool and are awarded their promise badge. There are then three journeys of challenge: Footpath 7-8 years; Roadway 8-9 years; Highway 9-10 years. There are many badges the girls can work for (69 at the present time) individually or as a pack.

The Guider will encourage the girls to work together as a whole pack or in sixes, develop physical fitness, develop relationships with each other and generally care for others. The girls will make their own decisions in groups called pow wow.

There are certain ceremonies each meeting and the Brownies attend Church Parade once a month. The Brownies meetings are usually full of fun as well as challenge and the girls enjoy raising funds for others less fortunate than themselves.

NATURAL HISTORY

West Sedgemoor

West Sedgemoor is a nationally important area of low-lying wet meadows, including an extensive area of unimproved herb-rich hay meadows and pastures. The meadows lie in an enclosed basin lined with marine clay, overlain with peat to a typical depth of 5 m, with further deposits of clay in some parts. Prior to drainage it was inundated with freshwater flooding. The major water source rose in the Blackdowns and entered the area at Helland. The other main source was from tidal flooding from the River Parrett.

After embankments were built on the River Parrett in the 13th century, the water from Helland flowed through West Sedgemoor via a series of pools and into the river through sluices. The area was common land with rough summer pasture grazing and much permanent swamp.

The present pattern of field drains was produced by the enclosure of the land and co-ordinated drainage begun in 1816. The area still flooded regularly and was a freshwater lake for much of the year. Until a pumping station was opened at Stathe in 1944, the land could still only be grazed in very dry summers. Further pumping and draining schemes enabled many parts to be farmed like any other non-wetland area, although this led to a decline in conservation value, particularly for overwintering and breeding birds.

The RSPB began buying land here in 1979 and now own a large part of West Sedgemoor in the parish of Fivehead, along with areas of scarp woodland. The wetland policy has been to return to winter flooding, with a high water table during the breeding season for waders, followed by traditional haymaking and grazing. The aim is to maintain an internationally important site with large populations of overwintering wildfowl and breeding waders, with important communities of vegetation and invertebrates. Already recorded are 327 species of plant, 245 species of aquatic invertebrate, and 169 species of bird with 88 of these species, including 5 of waders, breeding in this area.

The woodlands on the south side of West Sedgemoor are part of a chain stretching 30 km from Langport to the Blackdowns. They consist largely of the traditional hazel coppice with oak and ash standards but also contain cherry, crab apple, wild service and small leaved lime. Owing to the decline in coppicing since the end of the 19th century, their conservation value has declined, but parts of them are designated as sites of Special Scientific Interest because they still contain some important species. There is an important heronry in Swell Woods with about 100 breeding pairs. This can be viewed from the hide next to the car park, just off the A378 near Swell.

Wildflowers

West Sedgemoor

The rhynes contain the plants of the original marsh, whilst the deep water drains maintain the "pool" flora such as duckweeds. The shallow waters have plants such as water violet, while the water's edge has "emergent" species such as bullrush, water mint and marsh horsetail. All these plants rely on the condition of the rhynes and the cycle of non-chemical clearance to keep a variety of habitats and to enable recolonisation from one area to another.

The plants found in the meadows have descended from the original marsh plants. As well as well-known flowers such as ragged robin, marsh orchid and marsh marigold, there may be another 40 species in a typical field. The type of plant depends on the field's management; a hay meadow cut in mid July contains tall flowering species like meadowsweet, yellow iris and angelica, while a grazed field suits straggling plants like birds foot trefoil. All the flowering meadows depend on being regularly flooded with only the minimal use of fertilisers and herbicides.

Chilly Copse and surrounding fields

A survey of wood, field and hedgerow flowers in this area was carried out by Joan Greenshields over one complete year. The following list shows those positively identified; there are many more yet to be found.

First seen from March to April: daisy, wood anemone, dog violet, woodruff, wild strawberry, celandine, buttercup, bluebell, lords & ladies, stitchwort, dogs mercury, primrose, cowslip, forget-me-not, mouse-ear chickweed & spurge.

First seen in May: speedwell, pignut, clover - white & red, greater butterfly orchid, yellow archangel, bladder campion, meadow vetchling (Somerset name - old grannie slipper-slopper), bugle, cut leaved geranium, ragged robin, spotted orchid, scarlet pimpernel, convolvulus, vetch, bitter sweet or woody nightshade, blackberry, herb robert, cow parsley & stinking iris or gladdon.

First seen in June and July: tway blade, meadow sweet, betony, scabious, dog rose, ragwort, self-heal & old man's beard.

Fivehead arable fields

These three fields on the western edge of the parish were made a site of Special Scientific Interest by English Nature because the 25 acre "site has one of the most important assemblages of arable weeds in Britain". They have been owned by Somerset Wildlife Trust since 1992.

The rare weeds that grow here must have fitted in with the farming practised on these fields. The calcareous clay soil would only have been suitable for cultivation during a short period of time in Autumn, while these weeds set their seed after mid August but germinate before mid November. Their continued survival means that the fields must have been regularly cultivated, never pasture, and there must have been little, if any, use of herbicides or fertilizers.

Amongst the rare weeds are: Corn parsley; broad-leaved spurge; spreading hedge parsley, plus three Red Data Book species; corn buttercup; shepherds needle; broad-fruited cornsalad.

Teazels

The growing of teazels, which, owing to the type of ground, was a very local industry, has now almost disappeared. Seed was sown late March or early April, often using a variety called Dipsacus Fullonum, and kept free of weeds by hoeing until November. The plants would then be pulled and put into piles to await being carted away by horse and putt, a small almost square cart, to the area where they were planted for their permanent life. This planting had to be finished by Christmas, and they would still be kept weed free if possible till the following July/August, when the teazels would have formed and bloomed, the flowers covering the whole of the head with a pale mauve haze.

The largest teazel in the centre of the plant was called the "king" and these would bloom first and be cut first. As some of the plants would be about 6 ft tall, it was an arm aching job to cut them, and this was done individually with a small crescent shaped knife, which was tied on to the right hand glove. A sturdy leather pair of gloves was need to protect the skin from the many prickles of the stems. Also an old coat or mackintosh was worn to protect other clothing, as the stems exuded a black juice, which made any material hard, and was also poisonous to any cut fingers.

The teazels had to be counted as they were cut, and a handful of either 40 or 50 were then bound with a long stemmed teazel pushed through the handful, and the end put under the bind to secure it. Handfuls would be put into heaps in the rows, until the evening, when the children would help by handing the handfuls to the cutters to be placed on long poles for drying. This was called lugging, and when rain was imminent, or lots of poles were ready, they would be hauled to an open-sided shed so that they could finish drying. A pack consisted of 20,000 teazels, and it was on this amount that cutters would be paid. A good cutter would cut ½ to ¾ pack a day, depending on the time put in, but it was tedious work standing in the a very hot sun during August, with the added burden of extra clothing.

The teazel crop had to be gone over at least three times, and the last cut of the season would take account of all the small ones, so that cutting would be speeded up. As well as being dried indoors, when the weather was fine, gallows would be erected in the field, and the long poles of teazels would be placed against them, so that by partially drying, they would be lighter to carry to the sheds. Rain was the biggest bugbear to the teazel crop, and most farmers kept a "waterglass" to forecast the weather, as rain would soon rot the teazels and they would be useless. Sometimes a farmer and a teazel-man would form a partnership, the farmer providing the land, sheds, horses and wagons, with the teazel-man doing the hoeing, planting, cutting and hiring any extra cutters needed. The crop drew so much goodness from the ground, that they could only be grown in the same patch once in seven years. After the drying season, about September or early October, buyers would come from Yorkshire to examine the crop, as the teazels were used in the manufacture of good quality cloth, to bring up the "nap", and usually the seller was given a suit length of cloth from the mills. After a sale was agreed, large sheets would be sent to pack the teazels in, after all the seed was shaken out, as this would be needed to grow the next seasons crop, or, if not required it could be sold for bird seed for example. The packed sheets were then loaded onto wagons and taken to the nearest GWR station for the start of their long journey North. The dried stalks left after the crop had been cut, were pulled up and tied into bundles, for use in the home as fire-lighters, or sometimes as a lining in a shed to provide extra shelter during the lamming season.

Some of the birds in Fivehead and Swell

The bird for which Fivehead is famous in ornithological circles must be the Grey Heron. Individuals may be seen in the area at any time wherever there are fish or frogs etc., to be caught, but there is a great influx when the birds return to the heronry in Swell Wood each year from February onwards. It is the sixth largest heronry in Britain and would seem to have been in existence for at least 100 years. The number of breeding pairs has increased over the past decade from 80 to 100, so at the moment the herons are doing well. In early spring as one drives along the road to and from Langport these majestic birds can frequently be seen carrying twigs towards their nesting site. From the RSPB car park one can hear the noise as the birds establish their individual territories. In earlier years the nests could be seen from the road, but now the nests are built much further into the woodland where there is an observation hide.

People in the village with fish in their ponds report visits from herons usually very early in the morning when all is quiet. These birds have also been seen catching frogs in the fields alongside the road which leads to Isle Brewers.

Another bird which is a feature of the parish is the Buzzard. A pair usually nests each year in Chilly Copse along Fivehead ridge and others are to be found in Fivehead woods. They like to use old crows' nests. There was a high population of these birds until about 1954 when, after a hard winter, many were killed because it was thought they were taking lambs. Now the population is on the increase. Some times in spring as many as a dozen may be seen wheeling in the sky together. The buzzard's main diet is the rabbit. When perched in a tree, or on a post, the bird is somewhat dull looking with brown upper parts and yellow legs. In the air, however, it looks as though it has effortless mastery of flight. It can be seen with broad wings and rounded tail as it soars majestically in wide spirals gaining height from the thermals.

Figure 26: Head of Buzzard (sketched by Jonathan Hanney)

The Nightingale is fortunately still to be found in good numbers in the woodland thickets along the north side of Fivehead ridge and along the South Drove. This summer visitor is a relative of the robin. It is very shy and not very often seen; but its song is well known for its magnificence. It sings during the day as well as at night and can usually be heard during May in Standerwick Lane. Occasionally it is heard singing in overgrown gardens near the village centre. But, as land has been cleared for development, this has become more of a rarity.

An account of Fivehead's birds would not be complete without including something concerning the reserve belonging to the Royal Society for the Protection of Birds on West

Sedgemoor. About one quarter of this area lies within the Parish of Fivehead and for many species its a place of national importance. For example, the skylark is a declining species in Britain, but is commonly to be found breeding on Sedgemoor in fair numbers, although it is absent for the rest of the year. Other birds which nest on the fields of the moor include the curlew, redshank, lapwing and snipe. Around 5 to 10 pairs of lapwings and the same number of snipe nested in 1997. These numbers are significant because these two birds are losing ground on a national level, on account of the increasing lack of suitable land on which to nest.

The hedgerows around the South Drove are dense and rich in wildlife. Because the vegetation can grow without being flailed back each year, it supports many summer migrant visitors eg blackcap, garden warbler, chiff chaff, willow warbler, whitethroat and lesser whitethroat. Another summer visitor is the hobby. This is a bird of prey which captures its food almost exclusively in the air. It feeds not only on small birds but also on insects, especially on newly emerged dragonflies.

In autumn and winter the scene changes. Thousands of waders such as lapwings and golden plover come to feed on the flooded grasslands. It is thought that the lapwings are not British birds but come mainly from the Low Countries. These are joined by wintering snipe, and ducks such as teal and widgeon, and also by a certain number of shoveller and pintail. This bonanza of winter birds attracts birds of prey such as juvenile peregrine falcons which now have to "go it alone", having dispersed from the security of their parents' nesting site.

Apart from all these outstanding birds there is quite a variety of other species to be found in Fivehead. Many people feed the birds in their gardens and this must help the birds to keep up their numbers, especially during hard winters. Feeding also attracts extra species. In an old apple orchard at Tudor Cottage near the village centre, 51 different kinds have been seen during the last five years. The tit family is well represented, with long tail tits starting to visit hanging peanut feeders. The marsh tit, although present in Swell Wood and in gardens near the main road to Langport, seems to be an absentee in the village centre. This also applies to the nuthatch. Despite the habitat being suited to it, is seldom seen. The treecreeper, on the other hand, does from time to time visit gardens which contain fairly large trees.

Many people have remarked on visits made to gardens by great spotted and green woodpeckers. Although the lesser spotted woodpecker has been seen in Curry Rivel it has yet to be sighted in Fivehead. It is thought not to breed in the area.

The barn owl is a rare British Bird these days. It is occasionally seen in the parish and is most likely to be seen in Swell. At the moment of writing (late August 1998), a Swell resident has heard three different species of owl calling: - the barn owl, the tawny owl and the little owl - all within one week.

Sparrowhawk numbers have increased nationally and there are frequent sightings in the village. One has to admire their speed, grace and ingenuity even when one feels sorry for the hapless smaller birds which are their victims. A sparrowhawk has been seen walking along the tops of garden hedges trying to make one of the sheltering birds "break" its cover. However this species doesn't have an easy time; those juveniles which have been unable to perfect their hunting skills die of starvation especially in winter.

Of the crow family the magpie has increased its numbers in recent years. This bird is not always welcome because of its attacks on other birds and their nests. Rooks are sometimes seen in the autumn picking up walnuts in the larger gardens and large flocks may be seen at this time feeding on grassland invertebrates.

Until the 1950s the collared dove was counted as a rare bird in Britain. It spread across Europe and first nested in Norfolk in 1955. From here it has spread through the country and is now one of our most common species. It is a handsome bird, but even if it is not seen, its presence is indicated by its distinctive call, which some people find somewhat monotonous.

Members of the thrush family are always welcome especially in winter when the resident blackbirds, song thrushes and mistle thrushes are joined by fieldfares and redwings. Between them they eat fallen apples and any other soft fruit that people put out. They also eat Pyracantha and Cotoneaster berries, of which there are many in the village.

Other visits to gardens in winter include the pied and grey wagtails, and an occasional white wagtail.

April and May see the return of the summer visitors. House martins and swallows nest on and in the Baptist chapel, and swifts can be seen in the evenings flying round the Parish church tower making their harsh screaming calls. All these birds are evocative of summer, as are the songs of the chiff chaff, cuckoo, blackcap and willow warbler.

Another welcome, but at first sight, insignificant looking bird is the spotted flycatcher. Its upright pose on a branch, with its short aerial sorties as it hunts for insects, makes its behaviour quite distinctive. This is a species with declining numbers and it joins the song thrush, bullfinch, reed bunting, corn bunting and skylark on the Red Data list of high conservation concern. The Red Data list means that breading numbers have declined by 50% or more over the past 25 years. Let's hope that these birds, which are under threat, and which are still sometimes seen in and around Fivehead, will be helped to regain their former numbers as we enter the new millennium.

Many thanks to Mr J Leece, the RSPB warden for Sedgemoor who has supplied additional data about the birds in that area, and also to Mrs M Hole and Mr W Saint for their helpful comments.

Some of Fivehead's mammals

Because we live in the countryside, and because part of the Sedgemoor Nature Reserve lies within Fivehead, not only is the area rich in bird life, but in mammals also. Some of these mammals, such as the otter and the dormouse, are classed as being rare on a national level, mainly due to the erosion of their natural habitats. So we are privileged to have them sharing our parish with us.

However, because birds are out and about during daylight hours it is relatively easy to see a number of different species. It is otherwise with the mammals. Nearly all off them are nocturnal and secretive, and avoid confrontation with human beings. This means that very often we are only aware of their presence by the various "signs" they leave behind.

Such animals are the fox and badger. We must all of us have seen their remains left by the roadside as a result of car accidents. The fox is less nocturnal than the badger for it can sometimes be seen slipping across a field, or the bottom of a garden or orchard. Sometimes their night time visits to our properties are all too obvious and for those who have poultry, the fox's visit can be most unwelcome! The fox is almost entirely carnivorous, and the droppings it may leave in the garden are dog-like and pointed. The badger is omnivorous. It will dig out nests of young rabbits and must play quite a large part in keeping the number of these animals down. Earthworms form an important part of its diet and it is the only animal brave enough to tackle wasps' nests. These it digs out with its powerful claws in order to eat the nutritious larvae. Badgers also eat various nuts and visit gardens in the autumn to forage for fallen fruit. It is then that we are most likely to notice their droppings. These are compact and their odour is not too offensive, being of musk-like quality. When the weather is cold, and food is difficult to come by, they root around in the woodlands for underground storage organs of plants, such as bluebell bulbs. Occasionally one may hear a badger fight going on in the small hours of the morning. This can be quite an eerie and bloodcurdling noise as it resembles a child screaming. The two badgers rapidly rotate as each tries to bite the other's rump.

Other garden visitors include the grey squirrel. This is not a native British mammal. It was introduced from N America only just over 100 years ago and has gradually replaced our native red squirrel. Although its antics in the garden are often enjoyed by many people, it is generally regarded as a pest; some even referring to it as a tree rat! The grey squirrel does serious damage to trees as it gnaws through the bark to get at the sap, and it will destroy nests of birds such as those of robins, blackbirds and song thrushes in order to eat the eggs or nestlings. Many people have problems trying to protect their bird feeders as the squirrel will gnaw through practically any material to reach the peanuts or other kind of bird food which they may contain.

Rabbits are a pest in several gardens in Fivehead, not only with their burrows, but because of the havoc they cause by eating vegetables and valuable specimen plants.

The smaller mammals are unlikely to be seen, unless one is a cat owner and the dead "offerings" are brought home for inspection! These include bank voles with their reddish brown fur, blunt snouts and small ears; and wood mice with their more greyish brown fur, pointed snouts and big ears. The former may sometimes be seen by day as they scurry across a path, for they can be active during daytime as well as at night. Woodmice, however, are entirely nocturnal and move by leaps and bounds instead of running as do the voles. Both animals eat seeds, nuts, insects and fruit such as blackberries.

The smallest mammals which exist in the area are the common shrew and even the smaller pygmy shrew. Their numbers are kept in control by predators which kill and eat them. Although the domestic cat will catch shrews, it seldom eats them because shrews have glands on their bodies which make them objectionable food items for the cat. Shrews can be recognised not only by their small size, but also by their very long, pointed and flexible snouts and their very small eyes. They are welcome inhabitants of the garden as they eat any invertebrates they can catch. These include earthworms, woodlice, insects, slugs and snails. Shrews are restless animals and are on the "go" nearly all the time, as they have to eat large quantities of food in order to remain alive. Their presence is often only indicated by the aggressive squeaks which they make when they encounter other shrews. However, human beings need very good hearing in order to be aware of these.

To the north of the parish are other mammals not found in the village centre. The woodlands here, such as Chilly Copse are of ancient origin, and are home to the roe deer. This is the smallest of our native deer, standing only just over 2 feet at the shoulder. It has practically no tail but a conspicuous rump, and a black muzzle. Roe deer are mainly nocturnal and are very shy. They are most likely to be seen at dawn or dusk when they are feeding. They can do a great deal of damage to trees and crops which are being grown near to the woodland's edge. Roses as well as brambles appear to be some of their favourite food items. Roe deer are also frequently seen in and around Swell. It is thought that they cross over from the woods on the north side of the main road.

The dormouse, mentioned before as being nationally important. It is found in the woodlands which contain coppiced hazel with an undergrowth of honeysuckle. Dormice use the honeysuckle to make their nests, and as they are good climbers, special nest boxes have been put up to encourage them to breed successfully. They are endearing little animals with yellowish brown fur, large eyes and a long thickly furred tail. Their diet consists mainly of hazel nuts and berries, especially blackberries, and also other vegetable matter. Dormice are the only British mammals which truly hibernate.

On Sedgemoor the otter is starting to make a come-back. A special group within the Somerset Wildlife Trust is monitoring its movements and its ability to survive. It is such a rare and secretive animal that only a few people in Britain have seen one. By all accounts otters are playful animals, making mud slides and then taking it in turn to toboggan down them. They have webbed feet and are very agile swimmers. Although their diet consists largely of fish, especially eels, they will eat any other animal they can catch such as frogs, waterside birds and voles etc.

It should be noted that there are also quite large colonies of brown hares on Sedgemoor. This is encouraging, as this animal is also becoming a rarity in Britain.

A mammal which may be found in the Fivehead and Swell is the bat which can be seen flying around on summer evenings. It is only recently that it has been discovered that many different kinds exist in the area, of which three may be found in Fivehead. The smallest is the Pipistrelle. This is quite happy to roost high up in houses, even in modern ones, and can squeeze through narrow gaps; sometimes slots less than 1/2 inch wide have been used. All that bats need is a fairly clean, quiet draught-free position in which to roost during the day. They do not harm the property in any way; any droppings which they leave are dry and have no odour, being composed only of the exoskeletons of insects and are therefore easily swept up and disposed of. The second bat to be found in the area is the brown long-eared bat. Its name describes its appearance and it particularly likes to roost on the roof beams. This bat can hover so that it is able to take insects, such as moths as they feed from flowers. The third bat, which may be seen in Fivehead, is larger than the other two. It has a large wing span, about the same as that of a blackbird, and some of these bats were seen one evening this spring (1998) coming out from one of the round holes in the gable of the Baptist Church. It is thought that these are probably Serotine bats, though it is difficult to be sure, as it is so difficult to identify bats unless one has them in the hand. All bats are protected by law as their roosting sites are under threat, and also there are fewer insects around these days. Bat conservation groups encourage people to provide suitable roosting sites in their roof spaces by leaving special entrance holes, and by putting up bat boxes on suitable trees.

Finally a word about hedgehogs. Some of the people who live in Fivehead have remarked that there seem to be fewer hedgehogs around now (1998) than there were ten or so years ago. Most people are pleased to have these little animals sharing the environment with us, especially gardeners, because hedgehogs love to eat food items such as slugs and snails. Incidently, there used to be many more hedgehog carcasses seen on the roads. As the motor car is one of the main cause's of hedgehog deaths, this would seem to indicate that there are fewer of them around. In any case, fewer ones are seen these days. Apart from road traffic, it is thought many die through eating food which has been killed with slug bait and other chemicals used on farm land. There are also fewer "green corridors" for them to move about in. Farmers tend to plough right up to the edges of hedges and, because of the housing boom, some of larger gardens have been used for property development. Both these things mean that there are fewer green areas in which hedgehogs can forage. It's a pity that the activities of human beings seem to pose the greatest threat to this likeable little animal. The only other animal likely to kill it is the badger, and then only in small numbers, as the badger can only catch the hedgehog if it is taken unawares, or if the hedgehog is very young and its muscles are unable to resist the badgers efforts to unroll it. It is suggested that we can help hedgehog survival, especially in the autumn when they need to be really well fed, by putting out cat or dog food (not milk), and by providing special boxes in which they can hibernate or breed.

Trees in Fivehead

The Churchyard and Cemetery

Trees are the biggest and longest lived of all living things on this planet. It is perhaps not surprising, therefore, that we often plant a tree to commemorate an important event, or think of trees as being fitting symbols of death and immortality.

Such a tree is the yew *(Taxus baccata)*. The yew is one of our three native conifers. Its foliage is dark and sombre and although it may not be graceful, nevertheless it has an air of strength and endurance and can live for up to 4000 years. There are very few trees of this age in the country and those which do exist have extremely wide hollow trunks, and are generally found in churchyards. This could be because the yew was venerated in pre-christian times, and it may have been planted at places of pagan worship before Christians built their churches on the same site. The churchyard in Fivehead has three yew trees. Of these, the one near the church door on the south side is a golden variety, and it is also very unusual in that it has a Cupressus growing up through its crown, probably because its seeds are wind borne. It has been recommended, by the South Somerset Tree Officer, that the tree is maintained in this form to preserve its unique feature. The other two yews are on the north side of the churchyard where they cast their symbols of strength and immortality over the tombstones. None of the three trees has a girth exceeding 9 feet which would indicate that they are still quite young in yew tree terms; probably between 100 and 150 years old.

The wood from the yew tree is both strong and elastic and is famous for its use in the manufacture of the English long bow. Before the battles of Crecy and Agincourt so many trees were felled that the supply became exhausted and timber had to be imported. The trees remaining today represent the poorer ones that were left, together with their descendants. It has recently been discovered that yew foliage can be used for cancer treatment, and some people save the clippings which can then be collected, so that the chemical Toxol may be extracted from the leaves.

The male and female flowers are born on separate trees. Although the seeds are poisonous, the scarlet fleshy part around them is not. These berries are sweet and provide autumnal food for thrushes, blackbirds and robins.

In the cemetery, towards the southern edge of the village stands a cedar which was planted in 1987 as a memorial of Queen Victoria's Diamond Jubilee. This is the **deodar** or **Indian cedar** *(Cedrus deodara)*. It is native to the W. Himalayas and was introduced into Britain in 1831. Its graceful downwardly curving young shoots and its evergreen needle-shaped leaves form a fitting centre piece for the cemetery. Immediately on the left hand side is an **everlasting** or **Holm Oak** *(Quercus ilex)*. It is native to Mediterranean lands and was introduced to Britain over 400 years ago. Most oaks are deciduous, but this one, as one of its names implies, is evergreen, and like the yew it is very long lived, which again makes it a fitting symbol for a cemetery. Because the holm oak keeps its lower branches it is as wide as it is tall and so looks more like a huge bush than a timber tree.

On the same side as the Holm Oak is a **Monterey pine** *(Pinus radiata)*. This was successfully introduced into Britain in 1833 from Monterey in California. It is a decorative tree with its "needles" in bunches of three, and is easily identified by its lopsided cones which may remain on the tree for many years. It is very quick growing, and in New Zealand it is a major timber tree for paper pulp, but not here.

Other Species of trees in Fivehead Parish

The Walnut *(Juglans regia)* is a handsome tree with a broad crown and is very attractive in spring as its bronze coloured leaves emerge. It has always been highly prized. The latin name *Juglans* is a contraction of *Jovis glans* meaning the nut of Jupiter, indicating that it was fitting food for the "King" of the Gods. The Romans used the nuts for food and as a source of cooking oil. The walnut is a native of SE Europe and Asia Minor and was introduced into Britain in early times - some say by the Romans. It is certain that it was established here by the middle of the 16th century when it was commonly to be seen in orchards and in fields near highways. The walnut has often been planted near farmhouses where its edible nuts would make a welcome addition to the people's winter diet, both as dried nuts and pickled when green. Perhaps this explains why many of these trees are to be found today in the larger gardens which are in the centre of the village, as many of the older properties were originally farmhouses with their attached orchards. Some of these walnut trees are considered to be of amenity value to the village and the council has placed Tree Protection Orders on them, so that they may not be cut down without permission. Provided there are no late frosts to spoil the crop, and the summers are not too cold, these trees can produce a good harvest. Surplus nuts are often sold in the village shop and at sales of autumn produce.

The flowers of the walnut have separate male and female parts, which are borne on the same tree. The male catkins are 2 to 4 inches long and are particularly noticeable when they emerge in mid-May. The wood of the tree has always been highly valued. It combines toughness with lightness and, besides its use for furniture, is used for making the stocks of guns and rifles. So many fine trees were cut down to supply the needs of Wellington's army during the Peninsular War, that our forests were denuded of more than two thirds of their walnut trees. All the juices of the tree contain a brown pigment, and when one peels away the green covering around the nut, one has to be careful not to get one's fingers stained.

The Ash *(Fraxinus excelsior)*, along with the oak is one of our most well known native trees. Several may be seen in the village between the Crown Inn and the beginning of Silver Street. Although the leaves, like those of the walnut, are divided into leaflets, the ash is quite different in habit from the walnut, being a tall-domed tree. The branches are widely spaced and leave the trunk at narrow angles. Thus the crown is light and open and there is a long clear bole up to the first branch. In the spring the ash is one of the last of all our trees to come into leaf. The flowers open in April, and as the twigs are bare they can readily be seen. They appear as globular purplish bunches along last year's shoots, the latter with their typical black squat leaf buds still waiting to open. The male flowers are set more densely than the female flowers. Sometimes there are separate male and female tress, and sometimes there is a mixture of both types of flower on the same tree.

The fruits of the ash form bunches or "keys" of single winged seeds, and they often hang on the tree well after leaf-fall. These seeds, which are a favourite food of the bullfinch, are efficiently dispersed by the wind, often well away from the parent tree. We must all of us in Fivehead have found self-sown seedlings appearing in our gardens from time to time.

In tree terms the ash is not very long lived; only about 200 years. Its timber is regarded as being at its best when the tree is 30-60 years old. The wood is strong and pliable and so will take great strains. It is used in the manufacture of oars, axe and hammer handles, hockey sticks and skis. The Anglo-Saxons used ash wood for their spear shafts, and during the 1914-18 war many ash trees were cut down for use in the manufacture of aeroplanes and gliders. Ash logs make good fire wood, and as Scouts and Guides who go camping know, it is about the only wood which will burn whilst it is still green.

The **True Service Tree** *(Sorbus domestica)*, which is on the side lawn of Tudor Cottage next to the churchyard is worthy of note, because although it is a native of Europe it is very uncommon in Britain. Its ash shaped leaves, and its bunches of whitish flowers show its relationship to the mountain ash or rowan *(Sorbus acuparia)*. There are two varieties; one with apple shaped fruits and the other with pear shaped fruits. The one in Fivehead has pear shaped fruits which are up to 1 inch long, green and tinged red to brownish when ripe. These are much enjoyed by winter thrushes and grey squirrels. They can also be used to make a cider-like drink; but, if eaten when not properly ripe they are somewhat poisonous having an adverse effect on the respiratory system.

The **English or Common Elm** *(Ulmus procera)*. This tall, narrow crowned stately tree, with its tier upon tier of graceful branches and billowing foliage was once a common sight in the Midlands and Southern England. Its origins remain enigmatic.

The elm was either an early introduction or may have arisen as a hybrid. The great landowners of the 17th and 18th centuries planted them as timber trees along the hedges and to enclose farmland, which probably accounts for their prevalence today along the sides of Fivehead's roads and lanes. Alas, now we only see but very poor specimens of their former glory, as they have all fallen victims to Dutch Elm disease. This disease reached Britain in 1967 when infected timber was imported from America. It is caused by a fungus which blocks the water conducting vessels in the branches and thus water and minerals cannot reach the leaves which then turn brown and die. The fungus is spread from tree to tree by the elm bark beetle. Of the 23 million elms which formed England's commonest tree, 17 million died. All that remains in Somerset are the skeletons of some elms which stand in bare tribute to their more illustrious past, and some "bushes" which have grown as suckers from the roots. When these reach a certain size they in turn succumb to the disease and in the following year show as dead spikes. Thus the disease recycles round. There was a resurgence in the early 1990s and again this year, 1998. The suckering habit is almost the only method of reproduction for the elm, as fertile seeds rarely set.

As a timber, it used to be in great demand, and was the least costly hardwood available. The old timber framed properties in the village are probably built with elm, as this was much used for this purpose in the early 17th century. Elm timber was especially suited for use where it would be in contact with water, and so was used for keel pieces on wooden ships and for water pipes before metal was used for this purpose. Some of these pipes lasted over 100 years. The palace at the Hague was built on elm piles, which are now several hundred years old.

Crack willow *(Salix fragilis)*. Of the smaller trees in the area this is one of the most notable. Its shoots are tough and pliant, but they can easily be snapped off at the base, and it is this characteristic which explains how its common and Latin names are derived. Crack willow is a native of Britain and is found especially in lowland areas lining river banks. Specimens may be seen in the parish by the Fivehead River near Two Bridges Farm. These trees have long penetrating roots which help to prevent soil erosion along the river banks. When its twigs are broken off they are often carried downstream, and where these become lodged, roots develop and new trees are established. This willow is perhaps most noticeable when it has been pollarded. It is "beheaded" when about 8 feet tall and a new crown of straight branches grows out. These are often harvested to provide straight poles eg, for hurdles. These yellowish shoots are particularly noticeable after leaf-fall and form a distinctive feature of the winter landscape in and around Fivehead and Sedgemoor.

The scarp woodlands of Fivehead Ridge and Swell Wood

These are part of a chain almost 20 miles long stretching from the Blackdown Hills and comprise a conservation area. These woodlands are of ancient origin, and oak, ash and hazel are the predominant trees. But among them are a few specimens of one of Britain's rarest native trees *viz* the **Wild Service Tree** *(Sorbus torminalis)*. Its leaves are maple shaped, but this is misleading as it is not a maple. Like its relative, the true service tree, it belongs to the mountain ash genus. Thus its flowers are hawthorn-like, and its rounded berries hang in clusters. These berries are brown and speckled rusty, instead of being a bright orange-red as are those of the mountain ash. In autumn the leaves of the wild service tree turn a purplish red. Hopefully, with careful management, this lovely tree will survive and grace Fivehead's scarp woodlands for many years to come.

Hedgerows

As, with most rural communities in Britain, the hedgerows in the Fivehead area are under threat. Up to 10% have disappeared in the six years between 1984 and 1990. They have been, and still are being removed to make way for arable crops and, of course, there is a large world population to sustain. However, our hedgerows have always been a feature of the countryside and form an important wildlife habitat. They are made up for the most part mainly of our native British species. Elm and willow have already been mentioned and we must all be familiar with the white flowers of blackthorn and wild cherry, which brighten up the lanes and the roadsides in early spring, to be followed later by the May blossom of the hawthorn. Other typical species include dogwood, elder, hazel, field maple, wild privet, spindle and various types of wild rose. All these not only provide cover for wildlife, but also rich pickings for food in autumn and winter. It's a pity that so many hedges have to be cut back before the fruits ripen. Let's hope that with good management, a sensible compromise between the needs of the human race and the needs of the other living things, which share our countryside with us, can be reached.

A SHORT HISTORY OF SWELL, IN SOMERSET

Swell

In William the Conqueror's Survey this place is written "Swelle" and described as being among the lands of Robert, Earl of Morton.

Swell is now a tiny hamlet in the Parish of Fivehead with Swell and is situated about half a mile south of the A378 Taunton/Langport road, and four miles west-south-west of Langport. Originally part of the hundred of ABDICK and BULSTONE, it is now in the electoral division of Yeovil, the County Court District of Langport, the rural deanery of Crewekerne and Ilminster, and the Diocese of Bath and Wells. In 1857 Swell and Fivehead became a united benefice but the parishes remained separate and distinct until they were amalgamated in 1933. In 1986 Curry Rivel also became part of the benefice, but each retains its own Parochial Church Council.

The area is principally an agricultural one, and although it has never been densely populated, only a handful of people live there now compared to its earlier days. It is interesting to note that in the 18th and 19th centuries there was little change in population. In 1971 for example there were 25 houses and 130 people in Swell and in 1822 there were 26 house and 28 families, 26 of whom were engaged in agricultural work either for themselves or more likely for the local squire.

Although a rural, scattered parish, a certain unity has been imposed on the community, especially in its earlier history, by the presence of a squire and his estate, and outlying farms and hamlets were knitted together in a common relationship even though he owned most of the land. The parish was undoubtedly further unified by the existence of the little church where people from the farms worshipped.

Its history is long, covering a period of well over a thousand years and although no earth shaking events have occurred there, the centuries have left their marks on it, notably in the ancient church and the mediaeval manor house. Its history can be followed through surviving documents and records connected with the Lords of the Manor and the church, and one can assume that the life led by the common folk was much the same in Swell as that of others in areas better documented. There are a few references, however, to indicate that Swell played its small part in English history especially as it affected the inhabitants. We are provided with names in some cases. In 1243 for example, one John Langespey murdered William de Westoure and as a result was declared an outlaw. John was "in the tithing of Swell, and its a mercy, he had no chattles"; but what happened to him, was he ever caught?, was he executed?

In the period of the Black Death (13th Century) several of the clergy of Swell, among others, were carried away by the plague. During unsettled times over the centuries, Swell provided its quota of militiamen to be called up in times of emergency. Swell even possessed an excommunicated person in 1623 in William Bryant, and one wonders if he ever returned to the fold of the church, or indeed why he was excommunicated in the first place. We know that a complaint was made by John Sish in 1631 that he should be repaid for repairing Hay Bridge (it is still there to this day) at his expense; was he repaid? A village pond once existed, situated just to the east of what is known as Monk's Spring. There was a time when Swell had its own gunsmith (1851-61), its own parish clerk, and even a stone mason (1923-31) but they undoubtedly worked in the parish and did not enter into any outside commercial enterprise.

Upon looking at church records for baptisms, one notes the large number of base born children in Swell in the 16th and 17th centuries. Fortunately the priests appeared to be willing to baptise such children, but there is little evidence to indicate subsequent marriage between the parents.

These are but a few of the things we know of Swell's past and can only guess at the many incidents which must have taken place there. Of two things we can be certain however; that throughout its long history the principal industry has been agriculture, and that the majority of the population has been connected with it. We know that in 1815, 1816 and 1818 there were Enclosure Acts, especially regarding West Sedgemoor, but these had little effect on the population or farming methods as a whole. It appears that the principal crops through most of the latter years were wheat, beans and oats, although in recent years crops have become more diversified.

In March 1885, by Local Government Board Order, West Sedgemoor, formerly extra parochial, was annexed to the parish of Swell, and the following year part of the Oathe hamlet was transferred from Swell to Aller at about that time.

By 1900 there was a definite decrease in the population level, and the area under cultivation had nearly doubled. Until 1900, the area was a hand-made world, and people had a sense of place, of belonging somewhere and there was a greater sense of the family as an institution. "For a family to maintain itself", says Lewis Mumford, "it must have a permanent headquarters, a permanent gathering place". That is what most families still had in England. A perusal of church records of marriage, baptisms and burials as far back as 1559 will show the same family names appearing page after page until the 1900's, where names new to the district began to be recorded. Two events occurred which began to draw the people away from the land: the advent of more advanced agricultural methods and machinery, and the greater wages that could be earned in industry in the larger villages and towns. It is true that both occurred in England much earlier than 1900 but their effect was felt much later in rural areas.

In recent years, as in most places, there have been changes in Swell. There is no longer the Lord of the Manor or Squire, the last, Admiral Sir Reginald Ernle Erle Drax Plunket having sold by auction the whole of the estate in 1952 to private individuals. They in turn sold many of the farm cottages to newcomers, principally to retired people or those engaged in work other than farming. A handful of new houses have been built since the end of World War II and the total population now stands at 50. Farming is still the principal occupation in the parish but the "ancients" would not recognise the fields they once ploughed for most of the hedgerows and ditches have been removed. The destruction of trees by Dutch Elm disease further altered the landscape.

Mention has been made of the parts the church and the Lord of the Manor played in the local community throughout its history. The church still stands and plays its role in the lives of the local population.

Swell Court - The Manor House

The English manor house was an offshoot of feudalism, a system by which men received their land from kings and leaders on condition that they gave them services in war. Landholders were, in effect, little kings in their own land. They were usually nobles or knights, and their household servants and peasants who worked their lands were serfs or villeins, for the feudal system rested on a substratum of serfdom.

This feudal system, founded by the Normans, saw little change until it was weakened by the Black Death (1349) and came to an end with the War of the Roses (1450-71) when powerful barons killed and ruined each other and the county squires became the "upper class" in society.

Figure 27: Swell Court

Manors spanned several historical periods. The Normans had the Great Hall and used it as a common meeting and sleeping place for all, as well as serving as a court, dining room, reception room and theatre for strolling players - there seemed to be no limit to the function of the Great Hall. When they began to feel the need for privacy they built flanking wings which were used as service or sleeping areas. Although glass was very rare in 1180 and was not even made in England until the 15th century, the manor houses were not dark and dreary places as one might imagine - quite the contrary, with lofty ceilings and large windows, and walls covered by the tapestries which the ladies stitched zealously.

The Great Hall ceased to exist, however, when the feudal system ended and the buildings were cut up. They became, as Sir Francis Bacon said "uniform without though severally partitioned within". Fortunately Swell Court, built about 1450, probably on older foundations, retained its appearance and functioned with its Great Hall for the most part, until the 19th century when drastic internal alterations were made.

The name "Court" was undoubtedly given the house in its early days, or possibly to an earlier manor house on the same site, and seems to indicate that people had to appear there before the Lord of the Manor to express grievances or answer for crimes.

The outstanding principle of good design in a house is that its plan should be easily read from the elevations of the house and this is particularly applicable to Swell Court. It is an early type of defenceless manor house of the late 15th century, and an excellent example of its time. The unusual raised front garden is due to the slope of the ground on which the house is built. One should try to picture the garden before the yews acquired such mammoth proportions and almost killed the scale of the house. One must admit, however, that the yews do add a certain attraction to the scene as viewed from a southerly direction.

Undoubtedly the front door was originally a projecting porch leading into the screened vestibule with another door opposite which led into the courtyard to the rear of the house. The screen was on the left of the entrance and gave access to the Great Hall which was in the centre of the house and which reached approximately twenty feet to a vaulted ceiling, a truly magnificent apartment. From the Great Hall one entered the withdrawing room where there was, as usual in similar cases, a stairway which led to the bedroom above it. On the right of the vestibule was the Winter Parlour, a modern innovation and almost the first of its type in the district. Adjoining the Winter Parlour at Swell Court were the kitchens.

The Minstrels' Gallery was reached by a staircase situated in the Great Hall, and which also led to the Guest Room which was over the Winter Parlour. Unfortunately this rather charming picture was obliterated in the 19th century. The Great Hall was floored over the first floor level, the fine roof was plastered and the space gained was filled with bedrooms at the expense of what must have been a very beautiful room. Eventually the Great Hall windows were filled in half way up and divided in their length. Gables that had fallen were replaced by hipped roofs, covered with modern slate, making, in the opinion of one writer, a "prosaic finish of what was once a very beautiful house".

The land surrounding the house has been given over to intensive agriculture and the many farm labourers once employed in the fields have gone, replaced by the machinery of our time, but with a little imagination it is possible to capture much of the spirit of past centuries in this ancient hamlet.

St Catherine's Church

Although the Bruton Cartulary states that Sir Walter de Essele (Ashley) gave the church "for the good of his soul", along with sufficient land to endow it properly, to the monks of Bruton in 1175, there is insufficient evidence to support Sir Walter's knighthood, and the grant was made in 1221/22, not 1175 as it was confirmed by Josceline, Bishop of Bath, in the sixteenth year of his episcopate. The small church is dedicated to St Catherine of Alexandria, with a ground plan which, with the exception of the chancel, is as it was in 1150, when it was built.

A chantry was founded about 1250 by Mabel de Revel, Lady of the Manor of Swell. Her endowment comprised 90 acres of land. This was confirmed by Walter de Urtiaco, her grandson, who gave a further three acres and one perch of arable land and one acre of meadow to provide a lamp and wine for the daily said office at the altar of the church. In 1292 it was valued at four marks and a half.

The advowson and rector continued in possession of Bruton Priory until the dissolution of the monastery in 1539. The living was subsequently used to endow the Dean and Chapter of the newly founded Bristol Cathedral. The relationship has continued ever since.

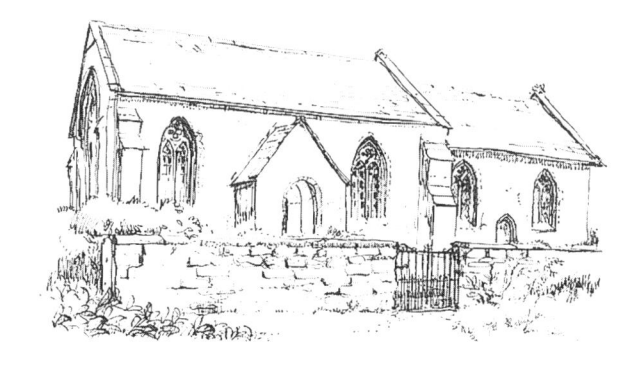

Figure 29: St Catherine's Church, Swell

Among bequests to the church appears one by William Grene, who by his will dated 1427 left 13s 4d to St Catherine's for an obit for the souls of himself, his wife Agnes, Agnes' first husband Robert Sparn and Elizabeth, Countess of Salisbury. In

1458 Edith Gaskyn left a gold ring with a stone to "the image of St Mary of Swell".

From the long list of rectors and vicars an interesting fact comes to light. William Porrett, MA, born in County Durham c.1562 and educated at St Alban Hall, Oxford, was instituted vicar on 5 January 1592/3. Although he gave way to John Wilkinson in 1622/23, Porrett was reinstated on 2 May 1623 and held the living throughout the Civil War and during the Commonwealth and was finally retired in 1668. Normally one would suspect that there had been a father followed by a son, but research discloses no other graduate MA of that name at either Oxford or Cambridge. It is doubtful that William would have retired at the age of one hundred and five years!

The present church, which may be described as a good example of perpendicular work, was in all probability built on the foundations of a Norman church and dates from c.1450. Except for a fine and rich example of a Norman doorway in the middle of the south wall of the nave and the font, which is either early English or Norman pared down, there is little left dating before the 15th century. The church was soon altered, however, by adding the present chancel, and an arch was inserted in the east wall of the nave to permit access to it. A small, pseudo-Norman door was built into the south wall of the chancel at the same time, and the piscina was added. The bowl is Early English and the two centred cusped arches above it are perpendicular or possibly earlier. At the same time the recessed niches, one on each side of the east window, were also added. One of these may have contained the image of St Mary.

During these alterations, the porch over the original Norman doorway was built, and the original Norman bell turret over the west window was replaced by a wooden one. All of the Norman windows were replaced with the present ones, many of which are glazed with the remains of very beautiful 15th century stained glass and old horny clear glass. Of especial interest in the east window is an angel holding a shield charged with the arms of Beauchamp of Hache (Hatch Beauchamp). Much of the original 15th century lead and iron work can still be seen in the windows.

Throughout its long history, it is natural that the church should have been restored or renovated. Many of the records covering the earlier years have been lost, and the first official record available is for the restoration of 1925. However, there is a reference in 1889 to a small stone bell gable with two bells above the west window which evidently supplanted, earlier in the 19th century, the wooden one erected in 1450. About 1900, after having helped to crush the mullions in the west window, this stone belfry, consisting of two lancet arches in the Early English style, was taken down and placed in the garden of the Rectory at Swell. Here it can still be seen in its original state in what is now the garden of The Old Rectory. The bells date back to the 15th century and are placed in the nave of the church. One is inscribed with a cross and the letters "Scanna", which is thought to be the stamp of the Bristol bell foundry of the 1400's, where it was made.

In 1924 it was found that with the settlement of the walls, the roofs had been subjected to such severe tension that they had been torn apart fibre by fibre. The roof was tied together by iron rods fitted to new wall plates, and although the sides of the building are obviously out of perpendicular, the fabric is safe. Upon completion of this restoration work, the church was re-opened for worship on 6 June 1925, having been unused for fifteen years.

In 1957 again much work was found to be necessary, and an appeal was made for funds. A grant of £330 was made by the Diocesan Board of Finance, and through the generosity of parishioners and friends £800 was eventually raised, and work commenced in October that year. It was at that time that the early 19th century elmwood box pews were removed because of serious decay due to woodworm. Those parts of any value were stripped of cream paint and integrated into the present pews. On 5 June 1958 the church was again re-opened for worship by the Bishop of Bath and Wells.

Both the pulpit and the remains of the prayer desk are good examples of Jacobean work, and the former bears the date 1634. The early oak benches are mostly in their original state and probably date from the early 15th and 16th centuries, as does the carved oak chest. The alter rail is probably later than James I. The benches were originally very plain, merely rough carpenter's work and were changed into their present state in the 1957 restoration.

In the sanctuary floor is a brass plate inscribed "Here lyeth the body of John Tooze Esquire, who was married to Agnes the daughter of Thomas Newton, Esquire having issue by her XIV sonnes and VI daughters. He deceased the X daye of June 1563".

There is an old money box bearing the date 1745 on the back of one of the pews near the entrance and appropriately, it is still used for gifts to the Fabric Fund. The church also possesses a very attractive traced silver communion cup and paten dated 1573, which are still used at the Eucharist.

The registers date from 1559 and are in safe keeping in the Somerset Records Office. They make interesting reading. From 1559 to 1625 the entries are in Latin, written on parchment in a beautiful copper plate script. Some of the earlier entries are now difficult to read, but the marriage entries have been transcribed and printed in Phillimore's Parish Register Series. There are numerous entries of deceased persons being buried in wool. (An enactment of Charles II was in force from 1678 to 1815; this was done to assist the growth of the woollen manufacturing industry).

In 1889 Mr Thackery Turner, the Secretary of the Society for the Protection of Ancient Buildings, visited St Catherine's and described it as not having lost its simple beauty over the years. As one sits today in the quiet of the church and reads his words it is clear that very little has essentially changed since 1889 nor indeed from the earliest days of this little church.

"This brief description gives but a poor idea of the real beauty and interest of this holy building. Upon entering it one is imbued with higher feelings and taken back in time through past ages. There are no modern vulgarisms to disturb one's quietness of mind, and as one sits studying the interior, one becomes more and more impressed by its great beauty. The absence of all violent colour, the quiet silvery grey of the old oak and the pleasant colouring of the pavement, the rich colouring of the windows with many beautiful fragments of old painted glass and homy clear glass, these I say, taken altogether, have a most charming effect. One may say briefly that the interior has just those qualities which are conspicuously absent in a restored church, and it is not only the interior of the building, for the exterior also has its charms. Unfortunately the original covering of the roof is gone, and has been replaced with the worst form of slating, but in spite of this the exterior possesses many charms, and it is much enhanced by the fine 15th century house which adjoins the churchyard".

CONCLUSION

The Parish of Fivehead and Swell has grown over the last 25 years to number 628 inhabitants. In the past the village was dependent on agriculture for its main livelihood. However with the modernisation and the mechanisation of the farming industry Many of the farms were sold off or merged, thus releasing land for infilling and small estates.

The majority of the working inhabitants commute to various surrounding towns and the children to neighbouring villages for their education.

Nevertheless the village remains in the main active with varied social activities such as the playing fields for the use of football, cricket, tennis and a childrens play area. There are also two churches, a local inn and a post office/shop. The local school was closed some twenty years ago and is now the village hall. It is used for such diverse activities as Play Group through to the Fellowship and Leisure Club with their chairobics and many more activities. The churches are used for appropriate events as well as places of worship; these include musical events, flower festivals and discussions. There is a surgery bus to Langport twice a week and fortnightly visits from the travelling library. Easter Sunday now sees a most successful Fun Run and August a Fun Day with something for everyone.

Whilst encompassing these changes Fivehead and Swell have retained their friendly rural community spirit.

Figure 29: Old threshing machine

The Bakery Fivehead 1900

Fivehead male Friendly Society formed in 1865. Picture taken in the yard of the Bakery around 1900. President Mr Frank Meade (Langport), later Mr WAK Matterson of Langford Manor. Secretary Mr E Gridley. The Emblem was a brass Dove on a pole with a bow of blue ribbon and blue rosette. The Dove was said to represent the bird which Noah sent out from the Ark. The Club motto was bear one anothers burdens. The Club Banner is now at Taunton museum. Club Day, the last Thursday in May.